KU-505-090

An Intermediate Guide to SPSS Programming
Using Syntax for Data Management

Sarah Boslaugh
Department of Pediatrics
Washington University School of Medicine, St. Louis

SAGE Publications
Thousand Oaks ■ London ■ New Delhi

For information:

Sage Publications, Inc.
2455 Teller Road
Thousand Oaks, California 91320
E-mail: order@sagepub.com

Sage Publications Ltd.
1 Oliver's Yard
55 City Road
London EC1Y 1SP
United Kingdom

Sage Publications India Pvt. Ltd.
B-42, Panchsheel Enclave
Post Box 4109
New Delhi 110 017 India

Printed in the United States of America

Library of Congress Cataloging-in-Publication Data

Boslaugh, Sarah.
An intermediate guide to SPSS programming: Using syntax for data management / Sarah Boslaugh.
    p. cm.
Includes bibliographical references and index.
ISBN 0-7619-3185-6
    1. SPSS for Windows. 2. Social sciences—Statistical methods—Computer programs. I. Title.
HA32.B67 2005
005.5'5—dc22

                                        2004014097

06   07   10 9 8 7 6 5 4 3 2

Acquisitions Editor:	Lisa Cuevas Shaw
Editorial Assistant:	Margo Beth Crouppen
Production Editor:	Melanie Birdsall
Copy Editor:	Carla Freeman
Typesetter:	C&M Digitals (P) Ltd.
Proofreader:	Teresa Herlinger
Cover Designer:	Michelle Kenny

Contents

Part V: Variables and Variable Manipulations

Preface

This book is about using SPSS to manage data. To be more specific, it presents a number of concepts important in data management and demonstrates how to carry out data management tasks using SPSS syntax. It presupposes no experience with data management, SPSS, or computer programming, but assumes the reader has the need or the desire to learn about those topics. It further assumes the reader has access to SPSS and to the *SPSS Syntax Reference Guide*, which is included as a PDF file with the SPSS software.

Data management includes everything necessary to prepare data for analysis, including

1. Getting the data into the computer program you will use to analyze it

2. Screening data for duplicate records, data errors, missing data, and so on

3. Combining and restructuring data files

4. Creating and recoding variables

5. Documenting the procedures performed on the data

People who work with data recognize that they often spend more time on data management tasks than they do performing analyses. Data management is often neglected in courses that introduce students to data analysis, leaving them unprepared to deal with data management issues when they begin working with real data. This book fills that gap by discussing common issues in data management and presenting techniques to deal with them. These tasks are accomplished using SPSS syntax, but the general principles can be applied using any programming language.

This book is also a basic introduction to SPSS and to SPSS syntax. This aspect will appeal particularly to two groups of people: those who currently use SPSS through the menu system only and those working in other programming languages who want to learn SPSS. Many important features of SPSS syntax are demonstrated throughout this book, and basic programming concepts such as vectors and loops are also introduced as means to accomplish data management tasks.

Part I

An Introduction to SPSS

CHAPTER 1

What Is SPSS?

A BRIEF HISTORY OF SPSS

SPSS is a statistical analysis package produced and sold by the multinational company SPSS Inc. SPSS was developed in the late 1960s by Norman H. Nie, C. Hadlai Hull, and Dale H. Brent. Their purpose was to develop "a software system based on the idea of using statistics to turn raw data into information essential to decision-making" (SPSS Inc., n.d., *About SPSS*, para. 2). Originally, the initials "SPSS" stood for "Statistical Package for the Social Sciences," but since the market for SPSS is much broader today, SPSS is now simply the name used for the product and company and not an acronym.

Because SPSS consists of a large collection of syntax written by different people at different times, terminology is not always consistent between procedures. Also, because new procedures have been added while older procedures have been retained, there are often multiple ways to achieve the same result. Neither situation is unique to SPSS, but they may be confusing to the beginning programmer. Neither, however, should present serious obstacles to learning SPSS syntax.

SPSS AS A HIGH-LEVEL PROGRAMMING LANGUAGE

All programming languages serve as an interface between the computer and the human being who wishes to use the computer to do something. Computer programmers typically speak of four *levels* or *generations* of computer languages, classified by distance between the syntax written by the programmer and the instructions executed by the computer. The first level is *machine code*, which is very close to the instructions executed by the computer, and very difficult for humans to learn. *Assembly language* is the second level, and general-purpose languages such as C are the third level. The fourth level refers to programs developed for a specific purpose or domain, such as SQL and SPSS (FOLDOC). The syntax of fourth-generation languages is far removed from the instructions executed by the computer, and they are easy to use because their syntax often resembles statements in human languages. For instance, you don't have to be an SPSS programmer to guess what the following program will do:

```
GET FILE = 'data.sav'.
SORT CASES by id.
FREQUENCIES VARIABLES = age sex race.
```

These commands will open a file called *data.sav*, sort it by the variable *id*, and produce tables showing the frequency of different values for the variables *age*, *sex*, and *race*.

SPSS AS A STATISTICAL ANALYSIS PACKAGE

Some people don't consider SPSS a programming language at all, but rather a *statistical analysis package* (Stone & Fox, 1997). This distinction emphasizes the specialized nature of SPSS and the limited options available when users want to go beyond the preprogrammed procedures provided. In fact, there is no question that SPSS was developed to perform particular data management and statistical tasks, and those origins are still evident in SPSS today. However, for most users, it is not a critical issue whether SPSS should be considered a programming language or a statistical analysis package. This book emphasizes efficient and flexible use of SPSS syntax to perform common procedures. The SPSS macro language discussed in Chapter 26 allows advanced users to go beyond the preprogrammed routines supplied with SPSS.

CHAPTER 2

Interacting With SPSS

This chapter discusses some basic aspects of using SPSS, including the following topics:

○ The SPSS session

○ SPSS windows

○ Basic rules about SPSS commands

○ Order of execution for SPSS commands

○ Interactive and batch mode

A warning: Some of this information is system-specific and will not apply to every installation of SPSS. Programmers not using SPSS on a Windows or Macintosh computer should seek further information from other users at their sites or from the SPSS manuals.

THE SPSS SESSION

An SPSS session begins when you open the SPSS program, and it ends when you shut down the program. This is an important concept because SPSS "remembers" certain things for the course of a session, then "forgets" them when the session ends. One example is the declaration of file locations with the **FILE HANDLE** command (discussed below): An alias associated with a location remains in force during an SPSS session but does not carry over from one session to the next. This has two implications:

1. In some versions of SPSS, it is not possible to change the location of a file handle during a session, and in others, it is possible, but a warning message will be issued.

2. **FILE HANDLE** commands must be executed in each session before the files referred to can be accessed.

SPSS WINDOWS

SPSS for Windows and Macintosh has a system of three windows that allow the user to open data sets, issue commands, and view output. These windows are

1. The Syntax Editor, which displays syntax files

2. The Data Editor, which displays the active data file

3. The Viewer or Draft Viewer window, which holds output produced during the session

The Data Editor has two parts:

1. The Data View window, which displays data from the active file in spreadsheet format

2. The Variable View window, which displays *metadata* or information about the data in the active file, such as variable names and labels, value labels, formats, and missing value indicators

When you begin an SPSS session, the Data Editor window opens automatically. Data files may be opened through the menu or with syntax, and you must have data in the Data Editor in order to execute most SPSS commands. When SPSS commands are issued, either from a syntax file or from the menu system, they are executed on the active data file (the one in the Data Editor) and results are sent to the Viewer window.

BASICS ABOUT SPSS COMMANDS

The name of an SPSS command is also the first word or words in the syntax specifying it: Examples of SPSS commands include **FREQUENCIES**, **COMPUTE**, and **GET DATA**. A synonym for command is *statement*, so we can refer to either a **COMPUTE** command or a **COMPUTE** statement.

Programmers also use the term *command* to mean the total set of elements necessary for a unit of syntax to run, including subcommands and variables. Subcommands, functions, and operators are referred to as *keywords* because they are a permanent part of the SPSS language, as opposed to variable and file names, which refer to a particular data set.

Most SPSS keywords can be abbreviated to three or four letters, so the commands **FREQ VAR** and **FREQUENCIES VARIABLES** will produce the same results. Shortened forms of commands are used frequently in this text. One exception is that the first word in multiword commands such as **FILE TYPE** generally cannot be abbreviated. SPSS is not case-sensitive when reading syntax, so **FREQ, freq,** and **Freq** will produce the same result.

Commands and subcommands may be included on the same line or on separate lines, so the following two examples of code will execute identically:

```
FREQ VAR = ALL / FORMAT = NOTABLE.
FREQ VAR = ALL
      / FORMAT = NOTABLE.
```

SPSS requires a delimiter between command elements: An *element* is anything other than punctuation that is required for a command, such as keywords and variable names. Usually spaces are used as delimiters, but commas or other symbols may be used. Multiple spaces can be used instead of one, and, with a few exceptions, commands may be continued over multiple lines. Subcommands are introduced by a slash (/). It is optional to put spaces before and after the slash, but they are included in this book to make the syntax easier to read. Similarly, it is not necessary to include spaces before and after the equals sign (=) in syntax, but they are included in this book for the sake of readability.

ORDER OF EXECUTION OF SPSS COMMANDS

In general, SPSS executes commands in the order they appear in the syntax file, so commands that read or create variables must precede those that manipulate them. Commands that perform statistical procedures and commands related to file management are executed as soon as they are read by the computer. Other commands, mainly those that transform data, are read but not executed until an **EXECUTE** statement or a command of the first type is executed. A third type of command, which affects only the data dictionary or settings, is executed immediately but will not cause data transformation commands to be executed. Lists of the first and third type of commands are included in the *SPSS 11.0 Syntax Reference Guide* (SPSS Inc., 2001), which also gives several syntax examples demonstrating how order of execution can trip up the unsuspecting programmer.

BATCH MODE AND INTERACTIVE MODE

There are two ways to submit syntax to a computer: *batch mode* and *interactive mode.* In batch mode, you prepare a syntax file, submit it in its entirety, and wait for the computer to return the results to you. In interactive mode, you submit small blocks of syntax, receive the results, edit the syntax, resubmit, and so on. Batch mode is the older way of submitting programs and is associated with mainframe systems. Interactive processing is the most common way to run SPSS on personal computers. SPSS can run programs in either batch or interactive mode, but there are a few differences in syntax rules. In batch mode programs,

1. Commands must begin in the first column, or a plus (+) or minus (–) symbol must appear in the first column.

2. If a command is longer than one line, the first column in each subsequent line must be blank.

3. Command terminators are not required.

4. Comments are indicated by an asterisk (*) in the first column.

In interactive mode programs,

1. Command terminators must be used (the default terminator is a period).

2. Most commands can begin in any column.

3. A command line may not be more than 80 characters, although a single command may continue over many lines.

4. Each command must start on a new line.

It is worth knowing the conventions of both modes, even if you work in only one, because you may need to adapt a program written for the other mode.

CHAPTER 3

Types of Files in SPSS

This chapter discusses the different types of files used and created in SPSS, including

○ Syntax files

○ Data files

○ Output files

○ The journal or log file

Some of the discussion in this chapter is necessarily system-specific: For instance, the syntax, data, and output windows are described as they are used in the Windows and Macintosh operating systems, as discussed in Chapter 2. The menu commands are also those for the Windows and Macintosh systems.

THE COMMAND OR SYNTAX FILES

A *syntax file* is a text document that contains SPSS commands. SPSS syntax files are identified by the extension *.sps*, so a syntax file associated with the project *base1* could be saved as *base1.sps*. Syntax files may be typed directly into the Syntax Editor window, also known as the *syntax window*, created using a text editor and pasted into the syntax window or generated through the menu system and pasted into the syntax window (as discussed in Chapter 5). You can submit SPSS syntax with the **RUN** button on the toolbar (it looks like an arrowhead in the Windows and Macintosh systems) or one of the **RUN** options from the menu.

THE ACTIVE OR WORKING DATA FILE

You need to have a data file open to use most of the features of SPSS. This reflects SPSS's origins as a statistical processor of data sets. When you open a data file in SPSS, it becomes the *working data file* or *active file* and SPSS commands will be executed on this data. There are three ways to get data into the Data Editor:

1. Include the data in a syntax file, in which case it is known as *inline data* (discussed in Chapter 8).

2. Type the data directly into the Data Editor window.

3. Store the data in a separate file that may be opened by executing syntax or through the menu system (discussed in Chapters 9, 10, and 11).

A data file consists of the data values plus *metadata*, which is information about the data such as variable names, value labels, and missing-data indicators. The Data Editor holds both types of data: The data values may be viewed by clicking on the Data View tab and the metadata by clicking on the Variable View tab.

In SPSS, you can have only one data file open at a time. When you open a new data file, the active file is closed (if it has been saved) or deleted (if not). When the active file is saved using a name and location already in use, the file previously stored at that location will be replaced by the new file, a process known as *writing over* a file. This is a problem if there is a mistake in the new file, for instance, if records were deleted unintentionally through the **SELECT** command, as discussed in Chapters 6 and 15. Experienced programmers use several techniques to protect against data loss. One is to make a copy of each data file they work with and store it separately from the copy used in their programs. Another is to periodically save intermediate versions of the active file with names such as *temp1, temp2,* and *temp3,* which indicate the order in which the intermediate files were created. SPSS system files use the extension *.sav,* and other types of data files use different extensions, as discussed in Chapter 12.

THE OUTPUT FILES

The Viewer window is opened automatically as soon as output is generated. *Viewer files,* often called *output files* because they store output from SPSS commands, are identified by the extension *.spo.* You may direct output to a

Draft Viewer file window instead: This window is text based and uses less sophisticated graphics. To direct output to the Draft Viewer, open a Draft Viewer window using the menu choices **File**, **New**, **Draft Output**, and output will automatically be sent there. Either the Viewer or Draft Viewer windows may be referred to as the *output window.*

The output window automatically displays the results of your program plus warning and error messages. You can also have syntax recorded in the output window by issuing the command **SET PRINTBACK = ON.** This is a good practice because it saves the commands that produce output directly before the output itself, allowing anyone looking at the output file to see how particular results were produced.

SPSS output files cannot be viewed by programs other than SPSS, which is a problem if you need to send results electronically (for instance, by e-mail) to people who do not have SPSS installed on their computers. There are several ways around this difficulty:

1. Save output from the Viewer window in portable document file (PDF) format.

2. Save output from the Viewer window in text format or rich text format (RTF).

3. Save output from the Draft Viewer window in text format or rich text format (RTF).

The principal advantage of using the first option is that everything in the output file, including charts, will be saved in the PDF document. To save a Viewer file as a PDF file, select **File, Print, Save As PDF** (Macintosh) or **File, Print, Adobe PDF** (Windows). A PDF file is identified by the extension *.pdf.* PDF files can be opened by Adobe Acrobat, a free software product that many people have installed on their computers (Adobe Systems Inc., n.d.).

Text files, identified by the extension *.txt,* can be opened by any word processor. The disadvantages of saving output in text format are that charts cannot be displayed and the appearance of tables may be quite crude. To save an output file as text, use the menu options **File, Export**. RTF files use the extension *.rtf* and can be opened by most word-processing systems. They cannot include charts, but their general appearance is more professional than the same output displayed as a text file. RTF format is the default option from the Draft Viewer window, so the menu choices to save an output file in this format are **File, Save**. To save an output file from the Viewer window in RTF format, use the menu choices **File, Export**.

THE JOURNAL FILES

The *journal file*, also known as the *log file*, records all commands and warning messages in chronological order from an SPSS session. It is a text file and can be opened with any text processor. Syntax can be cut and pasted from the journal file into the syntax window, as discussed in Chapter 5. The default name of the journal file is *spss.jnl*, and its default location varies by installation. You can change this with the **SET JOURNAL** command, so **SET JOURNAL base1** would cause the journal file to be written to the file *base1*. In some systems, you can choose whether the journal file will be *appended* or *overwritten*. If it is appended, the journal for each SPSS session will be collected in one large file. If the journal is overwritten, the journal for each session will replace or overwrite the journal for the previous session.

CHAPTER 4

Customizing the SPSS Environment

This chapter discusses ways to control the SPSS environment. Topics include

○ Displaying and changing current settings

○ Getting rid of page breaks

○ Increasing memory allocation

○ Changing the default format for numeric variables

Many settings or options are controlled through the menu system. Unfortunately, the sequence of menu items required to perform a task often differs from one version of SPSS to another and from one operating system to another. For that reason, this chapter deals with settings that can be changed through syntax. To learn more about the menu system for particular installations, consult other programmers using the same installation, the online help system, and the manuals included with SPSS.

DISPLAYING CURRENT SETTINGS

SPSS has a number of options that can be changed through syntax, usually by the **SET** command. To see all your current settings, use the command,

```
SHOW ALL.
```

The output from this command will be several pages long and in most cases gives you more information than you really want. The *SPSS 11.0 Syntax Reference Guide* (SPSS Inc., 2001) includes a list of settings that may be displayed and the keyword to request them, in the chapter on the **SHOW** command. This list is not exhaustive, however: For instance, the keyword **LICENSE**, used in the syntax below, is not included. To display a subset of settings, specify the appropriate keyword. For instance, to see the license number for your copy of SPSS, use the command,

```
SHOW LICENSE.
```

The output will display the license number, the components included and their expiration dates, and the maximum number of users.

CHANGING CURRENT SETTINGS

Most settings that can be displayed with the **SET** command can be changed with the **SHOW** command. The settings most likely to be changed by programmers are discussed below. Some settings are discussed in other chapters, including **SET JOURNAL** in Chapter 5, **SET HEADER** in Chapter 7, **SET SEED** in Chapter 18, and **SET EPOCH** in Chapter 24. In the **SET** command, the keywords **YES** and **ON** have equivalent meaning, as do **NO** and **OFF**. Therefore, **SET HEADER YES** and **SET HEADER ON** will achieve the same result, as will **SET JOURNAL OFF** and **SET JOURNAL NO**.

ELIMINATING PAGE BREAKS

The default page size in SPSS has a length of 59 lines and a width of 80 characters. You can see the current setting on your system with the command,

```
SHOW LENGTH WIDTH.
```

These settings may be changed with the **SET** command: Length can be any number from 40 to 999,999 lines, and width any number from

80 to 132 characters. If any length is specified, SPSS will insert page ejects at what it considers to be logical points in the output. However, some SPSS commands seem to spread output over more pages than is necessary. You can prevent this by changing the page length to infinite with the command,

```
SET LENGTH NONE.
```

INCREASING MEMORY ALLOCATION

Sometimes, you get an error message that an SPSS procedure could not be completed because of insufficient memory. At this point, you need to increase the memory allocation. Because increasing the allocation will slow down processing speed, you should increase memory allocation only after receiving such a warning message and restore it to the default setting when the procedure is completed. To increase memory for procedures such as **CROSSTABS** and **FREQUENCIES**, use **SET WORK-SPACE** to increase the allocation above the default 512 kilobytes. For instance,

```
SET WORKSPACE 800.
```

will increase this allocation to 800 kilobytes. If you get a warning message about insufficient memory to create a pivot table, use the **SET MXCELLS** command to increase it beyond the amount indicated in the warning message.

CHANGING THE DEFAULT
FORMAT FOR NUMERIC VARIABLES

The default print and write format for numeric variables is **F8.2** (floating-point or numeric format, with a width of eight characters, including two decimal places). Although you can specify formats through the **DATA LIST** command and the **FORMATS** command, sometimes it is more convenient to change the default format. For instance, you may have a file of responses to a questionnaire in which the only possible values are 1 through 5; it can be irritating to see them displayed as 1.00, 2.00, and so on. The command,

```
SET FORMAT F1.0.
```

will change the default format to **F1.0** (numeric format, with a width of one character and no decimal places).

Part II

An Introduction
to Computer
Programming With SPSS

CHAPTER 5

An Introduction to Computer Programming

This chapter discusses syntax and computer programming, including the following topics:

○ Using syntax versus the menu system

○ The process of writing and testing syntax

○ Typographical conventions used in this book

○ Presentation of code and output in this book

○ Advantages of using syntax

○ Ways to begin learning syntax

○ Programming style

USING SYNTAX VERSUS THE MENU SYSTEM

To use SPSS, you must have some way to communicate with the program. In colloquial terms, you need some way to tell SPSS what to do. There are two principal ways to communicate with SPSS: the menu system and syntax. The menu system is a graphical interface (also know as a *GUI*, or *Graphical User Interface*), which allows the user to make choices from a list. Many people begin using SPSS through the menu system, and even advanced programmers may use it from time to time. However, SPSS users beyond the beginning level often find that the flexibility they gain from using syntax greatly increases their productivity. Some advantages of using syntax are discussed in more detail later in this chapter.

THE PROCESS OF WRITING AND TESTING SYNTAX

Because many SPSS users do not have a background in computer programming, this section will introduce the vocabulary of computer programming and the basic process of testing and writing syntax. A computer program is a text file written in the syntax or code of a particular computer language. For instance, SPSS is a computer language, and when you write a program in SPSS, you use SPSS syntax. An SPSS program contains written instructions about what you want SPSS to do. To get SPSS to carry out your instructions, you need to submit the syntax to SPSS so it can be executed or run. Usually, running a program produces some kind of output, possibly with warnings or error messages if there were problems with the data or program. The programming process typically looks something like the following:

1. Write down what you want the program to do.

2. Write the SPSS syntax.

3. Submit the syntax.

4. Look at the output and find the errors.

5. Correct the syntax.

6. Resubmit the syntax.

7. Look at the output and find the errors.

8. Correct the syntax.

And so on! Step 1 is the most important: writing down what you want the program to do, in a series of logical steps. An example is given below:

Check the new data file for errors. This includes the following steps:
a. See how many cases are in the file.
b. See how much missing data there is.
c. See whether the data values are within acceptable ranges.
d. See whether the expected skip patterns exist.

A simple outline like this can be expanded to include more detail. For instance, it might specify the acceptable data ranges for sets of variables. You are much more likely to write a successful computer program if you have a clear idea what it should accomplish.

Programmers often speak of working for a "client," who is the person who wants the program written or the analysis performed. For instance, if you are a contractor, the client is the person or organization who hired you to perform a particular job. If you work in a company, the client may be your boss. If you are a student, the client may be your professor. Often, the client is yourself, in which case you have two tasks: Specify what the program needs to accomplish, and write the code to accomplish it. The process of specifying what needs to be done ("Check the new data file for errors" in the above example), including the necessary intermediate steps (points a–d above, the last three of which require further elaboration), can be useful for both client and programmer. This process increases the probability that the client will be happy with the final product and protects the programmer against the whims of clients who keep changing their minds.

TYPOGRAPHICAL CONVENTIONS USED IN THIS BOOK

Syntax will be presented in capital letters. Blocks of syntax is presented in shaded boxes. Syntax with the main text is presented in boldface type. Variable names, file names, and aliases appearing in the main text (i.e., not as part of a command) will be presented in lowercase type and italicized (e.g., *var1* and *file3*). SPSS error and warning messages will also be italicized. When incorrect syntax is presented for demonstration purposes, it will be followed by the symbol **[WRONG]**.

HOW CODE AND OUTPUT ARE PRESENTED IN THIS BOOK

This book emphasizes the commonalities of SPSS syntax across many operating systems. For this reason, system-specific information is avoided as much as possible. When system-specific information is necessary, it is identified as such and is presented as information for both the Windows and Macintosh operating systems. Output is presented in simple tables because the purpose is to show the logical result of syntax, not to reproduce the appearance of the Viewer window under some particular operating system.

SOME REASONS TO USE SYNTAX

Many college courses teach SPSS exclusively through the menu system, and this practice has created a generation of users with no experience in writing syntax. However, SPSS syntax is still widely used, and there are many advantages to using syntax rather than relying exclusively on the menu system. A few of the practical advantages include the following:

1. The syntax file preserves a record of the data management and analytical tasks performed on a file. Syntax can also include information such as when data were collected and at whose request particular procedures were performed, making the syntax file a repository of basic information about a project.

2. Sections of syntax or entire programs can be reused or modified. For instance, you may need to produce a standard report on a regular basis, a task easily accomplished by running the same basic syntax each time a report is needed. Similarly, syntax adding value labels to one data file may be applied to another file.

3. Most syntax will run on any installation of SPSS, while the menu system varies across versions and operating systems.

4. Syntax is an important means of communication among SPSS users. For instance, users often exchange code written to perform a particular procedure or solve a problem. Similarly, it is easy for one programmer to check another's syntax, correct the errors, and e-mail the corrected code back to the first programmer.

5. Many common procedures, such as recoding variables and computing new variables, are accomplished more efficiently through syntax rather than through the menu interface.

6. Some important commands, such as **LIST**, are available only through syntax.

Because many SPSS users are introduced to the language while studying at a university, it is worth noting some pedagogical advantages of using syntax. These include the following:

1. The discipline of writing a program requires the student to think of data management and analysis as an organized process rather than a disconnected series of procedures.

2. If students produce their homework by writing syntax, the resulting program serves as a record of how the results were produced and makes it easier for the professor to find the cause of any errors in the output.

3. Students often get lost when a procedure is demonstrated in class by rapid-fire clicking through the menus, whereas if they are provided with code, they can refer to it and modify it at their leisure.

4. Using and modifying simple syntax is an easy way to begin learning computer programming and can be a stepping-stone to more complex procedures, such as writing macros (discussed in Chapter 26).

BEGINNING TO LEARN SYNTAX

Most programmers learn to program by modifying existing code rather than by writing entire programs from scratch. You can follow this natural learning process by using the SPSS menu system to generate code, saving the code in a syntax file, and modifying it. When you select and execute commands from the SPSS menu system, SPSS generates syntax to perform the procedures selected. You can capture this syntax in two ways: by pasting it into a syntax file directly from the menu system or by having it echoed (repeated) in the journal file or Viewer (output) window and pasting it into a syntax file. The following steps will paste syntax from the menu into a syntax file:

1. Start SPSS and open a data file.

2. Request a procedure from the menu system.

3. Click on **Paste** in the dialog box.

If you have a syntax file open, the new syntax will be pasted into it; if not, SPSS will open a new syntax file and paste the syntax into it. A syntax file thus created can be saved through the menu system with the choices **File**, **Save**.

Two other options for saving SPSS syntax are to have it repeated in the output file (the file in the Viewer window) or the journal file. The former practice is particularly recommended because it preserves a record of the syntax immediately before the output created by it. To have syntax repeated or echoed in the Viewer window, execute the command,

```
SET PRINTBACK ON.
```

To have syntax repeated in the journal file, execute the command,

```
SET JOURNAL ON.
```

These commands may be cancelled with the commands,

```
SET PRINTBACK OFF.
```

and

```
SET JOURNAL OFF.
```

You can see whether your system is set to echo syntax in the Viewer window with the command,

```
SHOW PRINTBACK.
```

Oddly enough, there is no equivalent command to see whether syntax will be echoed in the journal; the command,

```
SHOW JOURNAL.                                        [WRONG]
```

is obsolete. The output and journal files are discussed further in Chapter 3. Text from either file can be cut and pasted into the syntax window, using keyboard commands or the **Edit** menu.

Using the menu system to generate syntax is not just for beginners. Experienced programmers often use this system when they are using an unfamiliar command. The syntax for statistical commands in particular can be quite long, so generating the correct syntax through the menu system is easier than typing it and avoids typing errors.

Another way to learn syntax is to copy and modify code from syntax files written by other programmers. The complete syntax examples in this book are intended to be used in this way: Type them into the syntax window, run them, observe the results, then make modifications and observe the changed results. Other sources of code include books, the SPSSX-L mailing list, and Web sites, all of which are discussed in Chapter 27.

PROGRAMMING STYLE

Writing computer programs is a means of communication and a creative endeavor, as well as a method to accomplish data management and analytical tasks. Therefore, programming style is partly a matter of individual preferences. However, there are some conventions that are recommended to the novice programmer. These include,

1. Begin each program with a few comment (nonexecuting) lines that include the name of the program, who wrote it, when it was written and updated, and what it does.

2. Define the primary data files immediately after these comments. Use of the **FILE HANDLE** command, as discussed in Chapter 8, is a good way to do this.

3. Write syntax in logical units, separated by blank or comment lines.

4. Use comments throughout the program to explain what the program is doing, when and why particular decisions were made, and so on.

5. Use indentation to delineate command structure, for instance, to clarify loops and commands that continue over several lines.

The ability to use blank lines, indentation, and so on varies from system to system, but the basic principle of using spacing to delineate the program's logic can be accomplished in some manner on any system. Documenting syntax files with comments is further discussed in Chapter 7.

CHAPTER 6

Programming Errors

This chapter discusses programming errors, including the following topics:

○ The difference between syntax errors and logical errors

○ The debugging process

○ Common syntax errors

○ Common logical errors

○ Changing the display of error and warning messages

○ Deciphering SPSS warning and error messages

Beginning programmers may want to read this chapter to get a basic overview of the debugging process, even if they are not familiar with the specific commands discussed, then return to it when they have more experience with syntax.

No one writes perfect computer programs every time, so identifying and correcting errors is part of the programming process. Mistakes in a computer program are colloquially called *bugs*, a usage often traced to an actual bug (a moth) that flew into a computer relay system and caused it to fail (FOLDOC). It is not unusual to spend more time debugging a program than it took to write it in the first place, so the novice programmer is advised to get used to the idea of spending a large proportion of programming time correcting errors in existing programs.

SYNTAX ERRORS AND LOGICAL ERRORS

There are two types of programming errors: *syntax* errors and *logical* errors. Syntax errors are mistakes made in SPSS commands and are relatively easy to find because SPSS will generate an error or warning message relating to the error and will not execute the command. Logical errors are more insidious because often, faulty code will execute without triggering error or warning messages and the only sign of the error is that the output is not what you expected. As the cliché goes, the computer does what you tell it to do, not what you want it to do, meaning that the computer executes the syntax you submit and unintended results are usually due to programmer error.

THE DEBUGGING PROCESS

Writing well-organized programs makes the debugging process easier, as will the following suggestions:

1. Be familiar with the data set before you start testing your code.

2. Look at the results of each section of code to be sure they are what you expect: The **LIST, FREQUENCIES,** and **CROSSTABS** commands are particularly useful in this regard. This may be facilitated by running code on a subset of the active file, for instance, by using the **SAMPLE** command (discussed in Chapter 18).

3. Test each section of code in sequence.

4. If you are really stuck, invent a small data set with values designed to test a troublesome section of code.

COMMON SPSS SYNTAX ERRORS

A relatively small number of mistakes account for the majority of syntax errors. Over time, programmers develop an awareness of what mistakes they are most likely to commit. For instance, I am sure that at least half my programming errors are due to typing mistakes. For programmers just starting out, I offer this unscientific list of seven common SPSS syntax errors:

1. *Typing mistakes.* This includes substituting capital O for the number 0, lowercase l for the numeral 1, and misspellings such as *va1* for *var1* and **FRQ** for **FREQ**.

2. *Unclosed comments.* Comments that are *opened* with an asterisk (*) must be *closed* with a period (.). If the period is omitted, SPSS considers everything in the syntax file from the * to the first period following to be a comment. For instance, in the following syntax, the first and second lines will both be read as comments, and the third line will not run because no data file has been opened.

```
* Frequencies on the baseline file          [WRONG]
GET FILE = baseline.
FREQ VAR = ALL.
```

3. *Unbalanced parentheses.* As a general rule, parentheses must be used in pairs. *Unbalanced* or *unclosed parentheses* mean that half of the pair is missing, as in the code below:

```
COMPUTE var5 = ((var1 + var2) / (var3
  + var4).                                  [WRONG]
```

4. *Unbalanced quotes.* Like parentheses, apostrophes and quotation marks (both referred to informally as "quotes") should generally be used in pairs. If the closing quote is omitted, SPSS does not know when to end the quote string. For instance, SPSS will assign the text string 'blue 3' as the label for value 2, because of the missing apostrophe after blue:

```
VAL LABELS var1 1 'red' 2 'blue 3 'yellow'. [WRONG]
```

5. *Failing to declare a string variable before using it.* String variables cannot be created in commands such as **COMPUTE**. Instead, they must be declared with the **STRING** command, as discussed in Chapters 19 and 21.

6. *Omitting quotation marks or apostrophes when referring to text strings.* Text strings must be enclosed in apostrophes or quotations marks or they will not be recognized as text. If *string1* is a string variable, the first syntax below is incorrect and the second is correct:

```
COMPUTE string1 = May.                          [WRONG]
COMPUTE string1 = "May".
```

7. *Unintentionally deleting data with the* **SELECT** *command.* By default, the **SELECT** command's effect is permanent, and cases not selected are deleted from the active file. If permanent selection is not intended, precede the **SELECT** with the **TEMPORARY** command. The difference is illustrated below:

```
* This is a temporary selection.
TEMPORARY.
SELECT IF (gender = 'M').
FREQUENCIES VARIABLES = ALL.

* This is a permanent selection.
SELECT IF (gender = 'M').
FREQUENCIES VARIABLES = ALL.
```

In the first example, the complete active file will be available after the **FREQUENCIES** command is executed, because the **TEMPORARY** command limits the effect of a selection to the first procedure executed after the selection. In the second example, only the cases with the value 'M' for gender will be available for further analysis, because cases with other values were deleted from the active file by the **SELECT** command.

FINDING LOGICAL ERRORS

A logical error is a mistake made in translating your intent for the program into the syntax you submit to the computer. Logical errors are more difficult to identify than syntax errors because, often, syntax containing logical errors will run and the errors become evident only when the results of that syntax (i.e., the output) are examined. Therefore, once your syntax runs without generating warning or error messages, you need to examine the output carefully to see whether it produced the results you intended. If it didn't, you should work through each section of syntax step by step, checking the code and its output against your intent.

CHANGING DEFAULT
ERROR AND WARNING SETTINGS

Programmers differ in how useful they find error and warning messages, and SPSS has several settings that control whether they are displayed. You can find out how your SPSS system is currently set with the command,

```
SHOW ERRORS / MXWARNS / UNDEFINED.
```

The setting **ERRORS = LISTING** (or **YES** or **ON**) means that error messages will be shown in the output, and **ERRORS = NONE** (or **NO** or **OFF**) means that they will not. **MXWARNS** tells you the maximum number of warnings and errors; the default setting is 10. **UNDEFINED = WARN** means that warning messages for undefined data will be displayed, while **UNDEFINED = NOWARN** means they will not.

These settings can be changed with the **SET** command. For instance, the following code sets the error listing "on", increases the maximum number of error and warning messages displayed to 100, and turns on the display of warning messages for undefined data:

```
SET ERRORS ON / MXWARNS = 100 / UNDEFINED = WARN.
```

DECIPHERING SPSS ERROR AND WARNING MESSAGES

The beginning programmer may be frustrated by the error and warning messages displayed by SPSS. These messages are sometimes more useful in helping you find the general location of an error than in identifying what is wrong with the syntax. This can be useful information, however, because it tells you which lines to examine. It is also helpful to scan the lines just preceding the line that was flagged by SPSS as containing an error. Often, a mistake in a previous line will cause a subsequent line to fail to execute.

CHAPTER 7

Documenting Syntax, Data, and Output Files

This chapter discusses ways to document SPSS syntax, data, and output files, including

○ Using comments to document syntax

○ Using comments to keep syntax from executing

○ Documenting a data file

○ Echoing text in the output file

○ Using titles and subtitles

USING COMMENTS IN SPSS PROGRAMS

An SPSS syntax file should be planned as a document to communicate with human beings as well as computers. One way to enhance the information value of a program is through the liberal use of *comments,* or nonexecuting lines, throughout the program. These comments can include notes about the program itself, the data sets used, the purpose of the analysis, and what each part of the program does. Such documentation serves at least three purposes:

1. It creates an archive of information about the project.

2. It explains the logic behind the syntax.

3. It encourages the programmer to plan the analysis as a series of logical steps.

One way to include comments in a syntax file is as separate lines preceded by an asterisk (*) and closed by the command terminator, which is usually a period (.). Comments may be continued over several lines. If a period is included within a comment, for instance, when specifying a file name, it must be enclosed in quotes so SPSS does not interpret it as a command terminator. The asterisk style of commenting is demonstrated in the following syntax:

```
* This program 'ch08.sps' includes the syntax for
  chapter 8 of the SPSS book.
* It was written by Sarah Boslaugh; begun 08-10-2003;
  last updated 3-26-2004.
```

Comments may also be included on command lines, in which case the comment is set between the symbols /* and */. The command terminator (.) comes *after* the comment, as in the following example:

```
IF hsgrad = 1 AND sex = 1 fhs = 1 /*Female High
  School graduates*/.
IF hsgrad = 1 AND sex = 2 mhs = 1 /*Male High School
  graduates*/.
```

USING COMMENTS TO PREVENT CODE FROM EXECUTING

A common use of commenting is to keep one or more lines of syntax from executing. You can temporarily "disable" syntax by putting an asterisk at the beginning of each command, turning it into a comment. When you want the code to run, delete the asterisks. This system of "commenting out" lines of code allows you to preserve a record of the syntax previously used on a data file but differentiates it from the syntax currently used.

DOCUMENTING A DATA FILE

To attach descriptive text to an SPSS system file, use the **DOCUMENT** command. The document thus created becomes part of the dictionary of the file, and new documentation can be appended at any time. The **DOCUMENT** command is demonstrated below:

```
DOCUMENT This file contains the data collected in the
  baseline phase of the School Safety Project. Data
  collection took place from Sept. 1, 2001, to May 1,
  2002. Data cleaning was completed on August 30, 2002.
```

Periods do not operate as command terminators within the **DOCU-MENT** command. Each document is saved with its date of creation, and all documents associated with a data file may be seen, along with their dates of creation, with the command,

```
DISPLAY DOCUMENTS.
```

The command,

```
DROP DOCUMENTS.
```

will delete all documents currently attached to the file but will not prevent new documents from being attached to it.

ECHOING TEXT IN THE OUTPUT FILE

Normally, it is a good practice to have syntax repeated in the output file, as discussed in Chapter 5. However, if you choose not to use this option, you can still document your output using the **ECHO** command, which will cause the text following it to appear in the output file. The text must be enclosed in apostrophes or quotation marks, as in the following example:

```
ECHO "Descriptive statistics on the baseline file".
```

The phrase **Descriptive statistics on the baseline file** will appear in the output file. The **ECHO** command is not documented in the SPSS online help systems or in the *SPSS System 11.0 Syntax Reference Guide* (SPSS Inc., 2001). However, it does work on SPSS System 11.0 for Macintosh and System 12.0 for Windows, so I recommend experimenting with it.

USING TITLES AND SUBTITLES

Using titles and subtitles is another way to document SPSS output. To see titles and subtitles, you must have the headers turned "on" by the command,

```
SET HEADER = YES.
```

A title may be as long as 60 characters and will appear on the first line of each page of output, justified to the left margin. If apostrophes are used in the title, the entire title must be enclosed in quotation marks, and if quotation marks are used in the title, it must be enclosed in apostrophes. An example of a basic **TITLE** command is,

```
TITLE Descriptive stats for the School Safety baseline
    data.
```

Each new title command overrides the previous title. To cancel a title (i.e., prevent a previously declared title from appearing), use the blank title command,

```
TITLE.
```

A subtitle appears on the second line of output, justified to the left margin. The same basic rules apply as for titles. The following syntax specifies a subtitle,

```
SUBTITLE For APHA presentation.
```

Subtitles are canceled by the blank subtitle command,

```
SUBTITLE.
```

Part III

Reading and Writing Data Files in SPSS

CHAPTER 8

Reading Raw Data in SPSS

This chapter discusses ways to read raw data in SPSS. Topics include

○ Reading inline and external data

○ Reading data in the **FIXED**, **FREE**, and **LIST** formats

○ Specifying the delimiter symbol

○ Reading aggregated data

○ Reading data with multiple lines per case

○ Using FORTRAN-like variable specifications

○ Using shortcuts for declaring variable formats

○ Specifying decimal values

The most common types of data used in SPSS are raw data, SPSS system and portable files, and data files produced by other programs, such as EXCEL or SAS. This chapter discusses reading raw data. Reading SPSS system and portable files is discussed in Chapter 9, and reading files produced by other programs in Chapter 10.

The simplest way to store data electronically, particularly if they may be shared among a number of different software packages, is as a raw data file, also known as a text or ASCII file. The term *raw data* refers to the fact that the data haven't been formatted for use with any particular program, so they are still in a raw or unprocessed state. The term *text file* refers to the fact that such files can be created and read by text processors. *ASCII* is an acronym for the American Standard Code for Information Interchange, a standard developed in the 1960s to provide a common code to expedite file sharing.

SPSS uses the **DATA LIST** command to open raw data files. This command has two main purposes: to specify the names, types, and locations of variables within the file, also known as specifying the *file layout;* and if an external file is used, to identify its location.

READING INLINE DATA

Data included in a syntax file are known as *inline data.* The commands **BEGIN DATA** and **END DATA** are used to read inline data, as demonstrated in the following example:

```
DATA LIST / ID 1-3 (A) Score1 5-7 Score2 9-11.
BEGIN DATA
001  100  99
002  86   88
003  93   89
END DATA.
LIST VAR = ALL.
```

The **DATA LIST** command identifies the file layout for the data that follow, using the **FIXED** format (discussed below), in which variables are identified by column location. The data are presented between the **BEGIN DATA** and **END DATA** commands. Note that there is no period following **BEGIN DATA**. Table 8.1 presents the output from the **LIST** command.

Table 8.1   Data Read With **FIXED** Format

ID	SCORE1	SCORE2
001	100	99
002	99	88
003	93	89

READING EXTERNAL DATA

Large data sets are usually stored in separate electronic files known as *external* files. An external file may be referred to by its location or *pathname*, or through an *alias* linked to its location. The correct way to specify file location differs according to the operating system in use and other local factors, so the programmer is advised to ask someone at his or her worksite or school how to do it. Examples of pathnames in this book are for the Windows and Macintosh systems because they are used by many SPSS programmers.

The Windows and Macintosh operating systems both use a hierarchical file structure made up of a series of *folders*, which may contain other folders or files. The pathname, also known as the *absolute pathname*, specifies the complete location of a file. A Windows pathname separates elements with the backslash (\), for instance,

```
C:\Documents and Settings\User 01\Desktop\Time Series\
   data1.sav.
```

A Macintosh pathname separates elements with the colon, for instance,

```
Macintosh HD:Users:Desktop:Sarah:TimeSeries:data1.sav.
```

It is possible to refer to a file by its pathname within SPSS syntax. For instance, the following syntax will open the data file stored at the specified location:

```
GET FILE = 'C:\Documents and Settings\Time Series\
   data1.sav'.
```

However, it is more convenient to associate an alias or name with the file location and use it to refer to the file. This is done with the **FILE HANDLE** command, as illustrated below:

```
FILE HANDLE ts1 name = 'C:\Documents and Settings\
   Time Series\data1.sav'.
GET FILE = ts1.
```

The **FILE HANDLE** command associates the alias **ts1** with the data file stored at **C:\Documents and Settings\Time Series\data1.sav**, and the **GET FILE** command uses the alias to open that file. An alias chosen by the programmer need be consistent only within a given program (i.e., it is not permanently attached to any file location). The rules for SPSS variable names (discussed in Chapter 19) apply to aliases, including the following:

1. They can be no longer than eight characters.

2. They must begin with a letter or one of the symbols $, #, or @.

3. They may contain only letters, numerals, periods, the underscore, and the symbols $, #, and @.

4. They may not contain embedded blanks.

Using file aliases has several advantages:

1. They are shorter and easier to type, and therefore less prone to typing errors.

2. If a file location changes or if you are adapting syntax written by someone else, you need change the pathnames only once, in the **FILE HANDLE** commands. The aliases do not need to be changed.

THE FIXED, FREE, AND LIST FORMATS

SPSS offers three ways to specify file layout in **DATA LIST**: **FIXED**, **FREE**, and **LIST**. In the **FIXED** format, which is the default, each variable is identified by column location. This format conceptualizes the data file as a rectangular grid, in which rows contain cases and groups of columns contain variables. Consider the tiny rectangular data set presented in Table 8.2. This file stores information about students and their test scores. Each row stores the information for one *case*, which in this example is one student. *Variables* are defined according to their column locations: The variable *id* appears in

Table 8.2   Rectangular Data Set

ID			EXAM1		EXAM2		EXAM3		
1	0	1	9	7	8	5	1	0	0
1	0	2	9	5	9	7		8	9

Columns 1 through 4, the variable *exam1* in Columns 5 through 7, the variable *exam2* in Columns 8 through 10, and the variable *exam3* in Columns 11 through 13. The first case has the *id* number 101 and grades of 97, 85, and 100 on the three exams.

We could read this data into SPSS with the following syntax:

```
DATA LIST / id 1-4 (A) exam1 5-7 exam2 8-10 exam3 11-13.
BEGIN DATA
101 97 85 100
102 95 97 89
END DATA.
LIST VAR = ALL.
```

Results from the **LIST** command are presented in Table 8.3.

Table 8.3   Rectangular Data Set (Table 8.2) Read With **FIXED** Format

ID	EXAM1	EXAM2	EXAM3
101	97	85	100
102	95	97	89

There are several points to remember about the **FIXED** format:

1. Alignment within a field is *not* critical for numeric variables. For instance, the value for *exam1* for the first case above could be entered anywhere within Columns 5 through 7 and would still be recognized as the value 97.

2. Alignment within a field *is* critical for string variables. The value for *id* for the first case above is entered in Columns 2 through 4, so it is stored with one leading blank, as "101". If it had been entered in Columns 1 through 3, it would have been stored as "101" with one trailing blank, and would be considered a different value by SPSS.

3. When a format is specified, only the *name* of the format is used, not the *width* of the variable. In this example, we identified the alphanumeric format for *id* with the keyword (**A**) but did not include the length (**4**), because that information is supplied by the column specification (**1–4**).

4. Blank lines between the **BEGIN DATA** and **END DATA** commands will be interpreted as a case with missing values on all variables.

5. Blank numeric fields will automatically be coded as missing.

6. Not all variables have to be defined, and they don't have to be defined in the order in which they appear in the file.

A second way to read raw data is with the **FREE** format, also known as reading *freefield* data. In this format, you do not specify the column locations of variables, but each variable must be separated by a *delimiter*, such as a blank space or a comma. The syntax uses the **FREE** format to read the same data set read above in the **FIXED** example:

```
DATA LIST FREE / id (A4) exam1 exam2 exam3.
BEGIN DATA
101 97 85 100
102 95 97 89
END DATA.
LIST VAR = ALL.
```

In the **FREE** format, SPSS reads the characters up to the first delimiter as the first variable, the characters up to the second delimiter as the second variable, and so on. This example uses blank spaces and line endings as delimiters. If no formats are specified, SPSS assumes all variables are numeric and assigns them the default format, in this case **F8.2**. This is evident in Table 8.4, which presents the output produced by the **LIST** command. It is identical to Table 8.3 except for the trailing zeros in *exam1*, *exam2*, and *exam3*.

Table 8.4   Data Read With **FREE** Format

ID	EXAM1	EXAM2	EXAM3
101	97.00	85.00	100.00
102	95.00	97.00	89.00

Several important points about the **FREE** format:

1. Data may be entered so multiple cases appear on one line, or a case may be spread over multiple lines.

2. Because the **FREE** format defines variables by sequence rather than by column location, all variables must be defined in the order in which they appear in the file.

3. If a format is specified, it must include both the format name and variable width, as in the **(A4)** format for *id* in the above example.

4. If the blank space is used as a delimiter, it cannot also be used to identify a missing value.

5. If the blank space is used as a delimiter, it doesn't matter how many appear in a row. Any number of blank spaces between a pair of variables constitutes a single delimiter.

6. If a blank space or a comma is used as a delimiter, values that contain either of those characters must be enclosed in quotation marks or apostrophes.

The sixth point is illustrated below. The **DATA LIST** command defines a data set with one variable, *name,* which is alphanumeric and has the length 20, as specified by **(A20)**:

```
DATA LIST FREE / name (A20).
BEGIN DATA
"Abraham Lincoln" George Washington 'Thomas Jefferson'
END DATA.
LIST VAR = ALL.
```

Output from the **LIST** command is presented in Table 8.5. The first and third cases were read correctly, because they were enclosed by quotation marks and apostrophes, respectively. The second case was read incorrectly: SPSS interpreted the blank between "George" and "Washington" as a delimiter, so "George" was read as the value of *name* for the second case and "Washington" as the value of *name* for the third case.

Table 8.5   Alphanumeric Variables With Blanks

NAME
Abraham Lincoln
George
Washington
Thomas Jefferson

The **LIST** format is similar to the **FREE** format: You do not specify column locations for variables, and each data value must be separated by a delimiter. However, in the **LIST** format, each case must begin on a new line and may not be longer than one line. The main advantage to using the **LIST** format is that it limits the damage done by data entry errors. If a data value is omitted in **FREE** format, every value following the omitted value will be read incorrectly, while in **LIST** format, only values following on the same line will be read incorrectly.

SPECIFYING THE DELIMITER SYMBOL

It is possible to specify a character other than a blank or comma as a delimiter. The delimiter character is named after the **FREE** or **LIST** specification, and any delimiter other than the **TAB** keyword must be enclosed in quotation marks and parentheses. The syntax below defines the dash (-) as the delimiter, then reads a small data set using it:

```
DATA LIST FREE ("-") / v1.
BEGIN DATA
111-22-3-4444-66
END DATA.
FORMAT v1 (F4.0).
LIST VAR = ALL.
```

Output from the **LIST** command is displayed in Table 8.6. When a character other than a blank space is used as a delimiter, two consecutive delimiters signify a missing value. In this example, the fifth case was

Table 8.6   Data Read With the Hyphen as the Delimiter

V1
111
22
3
4444
.
66

assigned the system-missing value for *v1* because there were two consecutive dashes between "4444" and "66."

READING AGGREGATED DATA WITH DATA LIST

Sometimes data are available only in aggregated form. You can use data in this form for some analyses by using the technique described below. Suppose you have access to the data in Table 8.7, which classify people by gender and whether or not they were referred for counseling. You can read this data into SPSS with the following syntax and analyze them using statistics appropriate to a 2×2 table. In this example, we request the χ^2 statistic:

```
DATA LIST FREE / row column freq.
BEGIN DATA
1 1 84 1 2 118
2 1 97 2 2 116
END DATA.
WEIGHT BY freq.
VARIABLE LABELS row 'Referral status'
    / column 'Gender'.
VALUE LABELS column 1 'Male' 2 'Female'
    / row 1 'Referred' 2 'Not referred'.
CROSSTABS row BY column / STATS = CHISQ.
```

Table 8.7   Aggregated Data

	Male	Female
Referred	84	118
Not Referred	97	116

Each cell in the table is identified by its row and column location, so the value 84 is in Row 1, Column 1, and the value 118 is in Row 1, Column 2. The command **WEIGHT BY freq** assigns the value of the *freq* variable (which is the value from the table) to each cell. The **VARIABLE LABELS** and **VALUE LABELS** commands supply labels to be used in the output, as discussed in Chapter 20. Output from the **CROSSTABS** command is presented in Tables 8.8 and 8.9:

Table 8.8   Crosstabulation Table Created From Aggregated Data

ROW Referral Status * COLUMN Gender Cross-Tabulation

		COLUMN Gender		
		1.00 Male	2.00 Female	Total
ROW Referral Status	1.00 Referred	84	118	202
	2.00 Not referred	97	116	213
Total		181	234	415

Table 8.9   Chi-Square Tests Performed on Aggregated Data

Chi-Square Tests	Value	df	Asymp. Sig. (2-sided)	Exact Sig. (2-sided)	Exact Sig. (1-sided)
Pearson Chi-Square	.660	1	.417		
Continuity Correction	.509	1	.476		
Likelihood Ratio	.660	1	.417		
Fisher's Exact Test				.430	.238
Linear-by-Linear Association	.658	1	.417		
N of Valid Cases	415				

READING DATA WITH MULTIPLE RECORDS PER CASE

If a data file has more than one line or record per case, it must be read with the **FIXED** format and the **DATA LIST** statement must specify the number of records per case and which record contains each variable that is defined. The following code specifies four records per case (**RECORDS = 4**) and that the variables defined are on the second and fourth records (**/ 2** and **/ 4**).

```
DATA LIST RECORDS = 4
    / 2 race 12 gender 14 / 4 hsgrad 3.
BEGIN DATA
```

```
000000000
0000000000010200
00000
0010000
END DATA.
LIST VAR = ALL.
```

This example has been clarified by including zeros in the columns that are not defined by the **DATA LIST** command: Those spaces could just as well be occupied by other data values or blanks. It is also possible to specify record location with slashes: Each slash not followed by variable specifications means to skip one line. This is demonstrated in the **DATA LIST** command below, which may be substituted into the program presented above:

```
DATA LIST RECORDS = 4
   /   / 2 race 12 gender 14 /   / 4 hsgrad 3.
```

Either syntax will produce the output presented in Table 8.10.

Table 8.10   Single Record Created From File With Multiple Records

RACE	GENDER	HSGRAD
1	2	1

USING FORTRAN-LIKE VARIABLE SPECIFICATIONS

The FORTRAN language uses an efficient method of specifying variable formats that is often used in other languages, including SPSS. Even if you do not use this method, you need to know how to interpret it in programs written by others. A FORTRAN-like format specification includes three elements: the type of variable, its width, and (for numeric variables) the number of decimal places. For instance, the format **F3.1** refers to a numeric variable of width 3, with one decimal place. Two other important FORTRAN specifications are **Tx** for "tab (skip) to the xth column" and **xX** for "skip x places." For instance, **T10** means "tab to the 10th column," and **5X** means "skip 5 columns from the current position." FORTRAN-like data specifications are demonstrated in the following syntax:

```
DATA LIST / id grade1 grade2 grade3
(T2, A3,3(1X,F3.0)).
BEGIN DATA
0001 97   98   99
0002 87   88   89
END DATA.
LIST VAR = ALL.
```

The variables names are listed first (**id grade1 grade2 grade3**), followed by the format specifications, in parentheses (**T1, A3,3(1X,F3.0)**). This syntax directs the computer to do the following:

1. Tab over one column, that is, from the first to the second column (**T1**).

2. Read the next three columns as a string variable (**A3**).

3. Read three variables by skipping one column before each variable, then read the next three columns as a numeric variable with no decimals (**3(1X,F3.0)**).

Output from the **LIST** command is presented in Table 8.11.

Table 8.11   Data Read With FORTRAN-Like Variable Specifications

ID	GRADE1	GRADE2	GRADE3
001	97	98	99
002	87	88	89

TWO SHORTCUTS FOR DECLARING VARIABLES WITH IDENTICAL FORMATS

Often, a data file includes contiguous variables that have the same format. You can use the **TO** keyword to refer to them in **DATA LIST** and other procedures:

```
DATA LIST / ID 1-2 (A) resp1 TO resp6 3-8.
BEGIN DATA
01110011
02101101
```

```
03100110
END DATA.
LIST VAR = ALL.
```

SPSS will allocate the columns specified (3–8 in this case) evenly to the number of variables specified (6, in this case), so *resp1* to *resp6* are read as numeric variables of length 1. Output from the **LIST** command is presented in Table 8.12.

Table 8.12   Data Read Using the *var1* to *varx* Convention

ID	RESP1	RESP2	RESP3	RESP4	RESP5	RESP6
01	1	1	0	0	1	1
02	1	0	1	1	0	1
03	1	0	0	1	1	0

A second way to declare a series of consecutive variables allows you to specify their format. This method is demonstrated in the syntax below:

```
DATA LIST / a1 TO a3 (3A2) n1 n2 (2F2.1).
BEGIN DATA
aabbcc1122
ddeeff3344
END DATA.
LIST VAR = ALL.
```

The **3** in (**3A2**) and the **2** in (**2F2.1**) are multipliers: They instruct SPSS to create three string variables of length 2 and two numeric variables of length 2, with one decimal place. Output from the **LIST** is presented in Table 8.13.

Table 8.13   Data Read Using Multipliers With Formats

A1	A2	A3	N1	N2
aa	bb	cc	1.1	2.2
dd	ee	ff	3.3	4.4

SPECIFYING DECIMAL VALUES IN DATA

There are several options for specifying decimal points in a data file. The simplest is to include them in the data itself, as in the following syntax:

```
DATA LIST FREE / id (A3) gpa.
BEGIN DATA
101 3.4
102 3.1
103 3.8
END DATA.
LIST VAR = ALL.
```

Output from the **LIST** command is displayed in Table 8.14.

Table 8.14   Data Read With Decimals Typed Into the Data Set

ID	GPA
101	3.40
102	3.10
103	3.80

The variable *gpa* appears with trailing zeros because it was read with the default **F8.2** format. Including variable formats in the **DATA LIST** command will prevent this, as is demonstrated in the following syntax:

```
DATA LIST FREE / id (A3) gpa (F3.1).
BEGIN DATA
101 3.4
102 3.1
103 3.8
END DATA.
LIST VAR = ALL.
```

The output from the **LIST** command is presented in Table 8.15.

Table 8.15   Data Read With Decimals Using the **F3.1** Format

ID	GPA
101	3.4
102	3.1
103	3.8

A third approach is to use the **FIXED** format and include the number of decimal places in parentheses, preceded by a comma, as in the following example:

```
DATA LIST / id 1-3 (A) gpa 5-6 (,1).
BEGIN DATA
101 34
102 31
103 38
END DATA.
LIST VAR = ALL.
```

The output from the **LIST** command is presented in Table 8.16.

Table 8.16   Data Read With Decimals Using the (.1) Specification

ID	GPA
101	3.4
102	3.1
103	3.8

CHAPTER 9

Reading SPSS System and Portable Files

This chapter discusses SPSS system and portable files, which are data files formatted specifically for use with SPSS. Topics covered include

○ Opening system and portable files

○ Renaming, dropping, and reordering variables when opening a file

An SPSS *system file* is a binary file created by SPSS that contains data and *metadata,* or information about the data. Metadata is sometimes referred to as the *data dictionary:* It includes information about the variables in the file, such as their names, locations, formats, missing-value indicators, and labels. SPSS system files are optimized for efficient processing in SPSS and are the most common way to store data to be analyzed in SPSS. System files use the *.sav* extension. Saving data as a system file is discussed in Chapter 12.

Sometimes, a system file saved in SPSS running on one operating system cannot be read by SPSS running on another operating system. SPSS portable files are character files used to transport data in this situation. Portable files use the *.por* extension and, like system files, contain both data and metadata. Saving data as a portable file is discussed in Chapter 12.

READING AN SPSS SYSTEM FILE

The **GET FILE** command is used to read an SPSS system file. This is demonstrated in the following syntax:

```
GET FILE = 'C:\Documents and Settings\User 01\Time
   Series\data1.sav'.
```

or

```
GET FILE = data1.
```

In the first example, the file is identified by its complete pathname, so the actual location where the file is stored is specified in the **GET FILE** command. When a pathname is specified, it must be enclosed in apostrophes or quotation marks. The second example uses an *alias*, which is a name linked to a file location through the **FILE HANDLE** command. Both means of identifying file location are discussed further in Chapter 8.

READING AN SPSS PORTABLE FILE

Portable files are read with the **IMPORT** command, as in the following example:

```
IMPORT FILE = base.
```

To open a portable file formatted for magnetic tape, add the **TYPE = TAPE** subcommand as follows:

```
IMPORT TYPE = TAPE / FILE = tapefile.
```

Details about transferring files through magnetic tape are discussed in the *SPSS 11.0 Syntax Reference Guide* (SPSS Inc., 2001), in the chapter on the **EXPORT** command.

DROPPING, REORDERING, AND RENAMING VARIABLES

By default, a **GET FILE** or **IMPORT FILE** command reads all the variables from a system file into the active file, in the order in which they appear in the original file and with the same names. A subset of variables may be selected with the **DROP** and **KEEP** subcommands. In the command,

```
GET FILE = base1
   / DROP = var1 var2 var3.
```

all variables from the file *base1* are read into the active file except *var1*, *var2*, and *var3*. In the command,

```
GET FILE = base1
   / KEEP = var4 var5 var6 var7.
```

only the variables *var4*, *var5*, *var6*, and *var7* are read into the active file. The **KEEP** subcommand may also be used to reorder variables. For instance, if the file *data1* contained the variables *v1*, *v2*, *v3*, and *v4*, the following syntax would read them into the active file in reverse order:

```
GET FILE = data1
   / KEEP = v4 v3 v2 v1.
```

Variables may be renamed within the **GET FILE** or **IMPORT FILE** command: The new names will apply to the active file, while names in the stored file will be unchanged. This is demonstrated in the syntax below:

```
GET FILE = base1
   / RENAME age = age1 grade = grade1.
```

The **MAP** subcommand produces a table of the variables in the active file and the corresponding variables in the system file. This table is particularly useful when you are renaming variables. The following syntax renames two variables and requests a variable table:

```
GET FILE = base1
   / RENAME age = age1 grade = grade1
   / MAP.
```

CHAPTER 10

Reading Data Files Created by Other Programs

This chapter discusses how to read data files in SPSS that were created by other programs. Topics include

○ Reading files created in Microsoft Excel

○ Using **GET TRANSLATE** to read other types of files

○ Reading data from database programs

○ Reading SAS data files

SPSS can open data files created in many common spreadsheet, database, and statistical applications. When SPSS does not have specific procedures to translate a data file from a particular program, the file can be saved as text data (discussed in Chapter 8) or as a tab-delimited file (opened with the **GET TRANSLATE** command, as discussed below), both of which can be read by SPSS.

READING MICROSOFT EXCEL FILES

Microsoft Excel organizes data in individual *spreadsheets*, which are called *worksheets* in the Excel system. Later versions of Excel (5.0 and higher) allow multiple worksheets to be organized into *workbooks*. Spreadsheets arrange data in a rectangular grid similar to that in the SPSS Data Editor, but they differ in several ways:

1. Row and column labels in Excel are included within the spreadsheet.

2. Often, cells within a spreadsheet are used for titles or other text.

SPSS can read column labels as variable names and incorporate them into the data dictionary. To avoid reading other nondata elements as part of a data file, there are two solutions:

1. Delete the nondata elements from the spreadsheet before bringing it into SPSS.

2. Specify the cells that contain data, using the **RANGE** subcommand, as discussed below.

READING DATA FROM EARLIER VERSIONS OF EXCEL

Excel 4 and earlier versions saved data as individual spreadsheets. The basic SPSS command to open an Excel spreadsheet from Version 4 or earlier is,

```
GET TRANSLATE FILE = exc01
    / TYPE = XLS
    / FIELDNAMES.
```

This syntax tells SPSS to open the Excel (**TYPE = XLS**) spreadsheet *exc01* (**FILE = exc01**) and read the first row of data as variable names (**FIELDNAMES**). If you want SPSS to read only a certain range of cells on the spreadsheet, specify this with the subcommand **RANGE**, for instance,

```
GET TRANSLATE FILE = exc01
    / TYPE = XLS
    / RANGE = F2:K25.
```

This **RANGE** command instructs SPSS to read data only in the rectangular area demarcated by cells **F2** and **K25**, using the Excel convention in which columns are identified by letters and rows by numbers. A range of cells is identified by the cell in the upper left of the range (**F2**), a colon (:), and the cell in the lower right of the range (**K25**). The **DROP**, **KEEP**, and **MAP** subcommands are available as with the **GET FILE** command, as discussed in Chapter 9.

READING DATA FROM LATER VERSIONS OF EXCEL

SPSS uses the **GET DATA** command to read data from workbooks created by Excel 5 and later versions. The procedure in this section will open a single worksheet from a workbook. The section on reading database files should be consulted if multiple worksheets from the same workbook will be read. If the worksheet to be read is not the first worksheet in the workbook, its name or position must be specified with the **SHEET** subcommand, as in the following syntax:

```
GET DATA
    / TYPE = XLS
    / FILE = exc01
    / SHEET = 2.
```

This syntax will open the second worksheet in the workbook *exc01*. Worksheets can also be identified by their names within the Excel workbook, for example, **SHEET = "First quarter grades."** If you want SPSS to read only particular cells within a spreadsheet, you must specify them with the **CELLRANGE** subcommand, which is analogous to the **RANGES** subcommand in **GET TRANSLATE**. By default, the **GET DATA** command reads the first line of the spreadsheet or the specified range as variable names. To prevent this, include the subcommand **READNAMES = OFF**. The following syntax reads the cells in the range **F3** to **P24** on the third sheet of the workbook *exc01* and does not read the first row as variable names:

```
GET DATA
    / TYPE = XLS
    / FILE = exc01
    / SHEET = INDEX 3
    / CELLRANGE = RANGE 'F3:P24'
    / READNAMES = OFF.
```

USING GET TRANSLATE TO READ OTHER TYPES OF FILES

SPSS uses **GET TRANSLATE** to read tab-delimited files as well as files created in Lotus 1-2-3, dBASE, and several other programs. Details about reading each type of data can be found in the *SPSS 11.0 Syntax Reference Guide* (SPSS Inc., 2001), in the chapter on the **GET TRANSLATE** command. Major differences in reading files from different programs include the following:

1. The **TYPE** command must be changed to agree with the type of file being opened. For instance, **TYPE = DBF** is used for dBASE files, and **TYPE = TAB** for tab-delimited files.

2. The details of specifying cell ranges differ for each program. For instance, Lotus 1-2-3 and Symphony files separate the outer cells of the range by two periods, for example (B2. .G30).

3. The number of variables that can be translated into SPSS varies from 256 to 128, depending on the program that created the file (Excel, Lotus 1-2-3, etc.).

READING DATA FROM DATABASE PROGRAMS

SPSS can read data from many database programs, using ODBC (Open DataBase Connectivity), including Access, FoxPro, Oracle, SQL Base, and SQL server. Either the **GET DATA / TYPE = ODBC** or the **GET CAPTURE** commands will allow you to read data from these and other database programs, assuming you have the appropriate drivers installed on your computer or server. The syntax required to open database files is complicated, particularly when data will be read from multiple tables. The easiest way to acquire the correct syntax is to bring the data into SPSS using the Database Wizard (choose **File, Open Database, New Query** from the menu) and paste the generated syntax into a syntax file. Further details are available in the *SPSS 11.0 Syntax Reference Guide* (SPSS Inc., 2001), in the chapters on the **GET TRANSLATE** and **GET CAPTURE** commands.

READING SAS DATA FILES

SPSS can read files saved as SAS data sets and SAS transport files, both referred to here as *SAS files*. There are two ways SAS manages files differently from SPSS:

1. SAS stores variables and value labels in separate files.

2. An SAS transport file may contain more than one data set.

The first point means that if you want to import value labels and output formats from SAS, you must specify the location of the formats file. This is only possible with SAS data sets; format specifications will be ignored with SAS transport files. The second point means that you must specify which data set in the transport file is to be opened. The basic syntax to open a SAS file is,

```
GET SAS DATA = 'sasdata'.
```

To open a formats file as well, use syntax similar to this:

```
GET SAS DATA = 'sasdata' / FORMATS = 'format1'.
```

where *format1* is the name of the file containing formats for *sasdata*. To open a data set other than the first within an SAS transport file, use syntax similar to this:

```
GET SAS DATA = 'sasdata' DSET(sas2).
```

where *sas2* is the name of the data set to be opened from the file *sasdata*.
SAS variables are translated to SPSS following these rules:

1. Numeric variables are converted to the default SPSS numeric format.

2. String variables are converted to string variables of the same length.

3. Date and time variables are converted to the equivalent date and time variables.

4. All SAS missing-value codes are converted to SPSS system-missing values.

If SAS formats are supplied, they are converted to SPSS value labels, with the following exceptions:

1. Labels over 60 characters in length are truncated.

2. Labels for string variables and noninteger numeric variables are ignored.

3. Labels assigned to a range of values are ignored, as well as those that use the SAS keywords **LOW, HIGH,** and **OTHER.**

Reading Complex Data Files

This chapter discusses ways to read nonstandard or complex data files, including the following topics:

○ Reading mixed data files

○ Reading grouped data files

○ Reading nested data files

○ Reading data in matrix format

Most data used for statistical analysis are arranged in rectangular form, in which rows represent cases and columns represent variables. This type of file is called a *rectangular file* because the data form a rectangle:

101156329123

102151683515

103273287261

This file layout is so common that other arrangements are referred to as *complex* or *nonstandard*. This chapter explains how to read data files arranged in several nonstandard formats.

READING MIXED DATA FILES

A *mixed* data file contains several types of records that include different variables and/or different locations for the same variables. The syntax that reads the file must identify each type of record and specify their file layouts separately. An example is given below:

```
* Reading a mixed data file.
FILE TYPE MIXED RECORD = rec 1.
RECORD TYPE 1.
DATA LIST / v1 2 v2 3.
RECORD TYPE 2.
DATA LIST / v1 6 v2 7.
END FILE TYPE.
BEGIN DATA
112
2    12
112
2    12
END DATA.
LIST VAR = ALL.
```

The file definition statements are enclosed between the **FILE TYPE** and **END FILE TYPE** commands. The subcommand **RECORD = rec 1** on the **FILE TYPE** command names the variable (**rec**) that will identify the record type for each line of data and its location on each line of data (**1**). This variable must occupy the same location on every line of data to be read and is not named on the **DATA LIST** statements. Each record type is identified by the **RECORD TYPE** command, followed by a **DATA LIST** command specifying the file layout for that type of record. Output from the **LIST** command is presented in Table 11.1.

Table 11.1   Data Read From a Mixed Data File

REC	V1	V2
1	1	2
2	1	2
1	1	2
2	1	2

It is necessary to specify only the record types that will be used. For instance, if we wanted to read only records of Type 1, we could delete the lines,

```
RECORD TYPE 2.
DATA LIST / id 2 v1 5 v2 6.
```

READING GROUPED DATA FILES

In a *grouped* data file, data for each case are spread over multiple records or lines of data, and some records may be missing or duplicated. SPSS builds a single record for each case, combining all the variables from the record types defined in the **FILE TYPE GROUPED** command, so variable names should not be duplicated across different record types. Reading a grouped file is demonstrated in the syntax below:

```
* Reading a grouped data file.
FILE TYPE GROUPED RECORD = rec 2 CASE = id 1.
RECORD TYPE 1.
DATA LIST / v1 3 v2 4.
RECORD TYPE 2.
DATA LIST / v3 5 v4 6.
END FILE TYPE.
BEGIN DATA
1112
12 88
12   34
2156
END DATA.
LIST VAR = id to v4.
```

When reading a grouped file, it is necessary to identify both case and record type on each line of data. The subcommand **RECORD = rec 2** names the variable that will identify the record type for each line of data (**rec**) and its location (**2**). The subcommand **CASE = id 1** names the variable that will identify each case (**id**) and its location (**1**). The **RECORD TYPE** and **DATA LIST** commands are necessary for each record type that will be read from the file. The output from the **LIST** command is presented in Table 11.2. SPSS read this file correctly, despite two irregularities:

1. The first case had three records, two of which were duplicates.

2. The second case did not have a record of Type 2.

Table 11.2   Data Read From a Grouped Data File

ID	V1	V2	V3	V4
1	1	2	3	4
2	5	6	.	.

A duplicate record within the grouped file type is defined as one that has the same record and case identifiers as another record; it does not necessarily have the same values for the other variables. In this file, Records 2 and 3 are duplicates. When SPSS reads a grouped filed with duplicate records, it retains the values from the record that occurs last in the file, in this case the values "3" and "4" for var3 and var4.

SPSS issued two warning messages after reading this data:

Warning # 517

A duplicate record has been found while building the indicated case. Each occurrence of the record has been processed, and the last occurrence will normally take precedence.

which pertains to the duplicate record for Case #1, and

Warning # 518

A record is missing from the indicated case. The variables defined on the record have been set to the system-missing value.

which refers to the fact that Case #2 does not have a record of Type 2. Neither warning will stop SPSS from processing the data, but indicates that you should check the data carefully.

READING NESTED DATA FILES

A *nested* data file has a hierarchical structure. Consider a data file with one set of records containing information about schools, a second set containing information about math classes within each school, and a third set containing information about students within the math classes. In this file, the highest-level record type is "school level" and the lowest-level record type is "student level." Each lower-level record can belong to only one upper-level group: For instance, students can be in only one math class, and math classes can be in only one school. Looking down the hierarchy, the opposite is true: Usually, a school will include multiple math classes, and math classes will include multiple students.

When reading nested data files, SPSS creates one case for each record at the lowest level, including information from the higher levels pertaining to that case. The data file must be sorted so records belonging to each case are contiguous and, within a case, are ordered from highest to lowest in the hierarchical structure. This is demonstrated in the syntax below:

```
* Reading a nested file.
* Students are nested within classes.
* Classes are nested within schools.
FILE TYPE NESTED RECORD = #rec 2 CASE = id 1.
RECORD TYPE 1.
DATA LIST / name 4-25 (A).
RECORD TYPE 2.
DATA LIST / class# 4-5 grade 7-8 size 10-12.
RECORD TYPE 3.
DATA LIST / stu# 4-5 gender 7 (A) score 9-11.
END FILE TYPE.
BEGIN DATA
11 Central High
12 1 11 35
13 1   M 95
13 2   M 86
13 3   F 97
12 2 11 32
13 1   F 95
13 2   M 93
END DATA.
LIST VAR = ALL.
```

As with grouped data, each record in a nested file must be identified by a record number (in this example, **#rec**) and a case number (in this example, **id**). SPSS created five records, one for each student. Each record includes information about the individual student, his or her class, and the school. This is evident in the output from the **LIST** command, presented in Table 11.3.

READING DATA IN MATRIX FORMAT

The **MATRIX DATA** command reads raw matrix data and converts them to a matrix data file that can be used as input to SPSS procedures such as **CLUSTER**, **FACTOR**, **ONEWAY**, **REGRESSION**, and **RELIABILITY**. A matrix

Table 11.3   Data Read From a Nested Data File

ID	NAME	CLASS#	GRADE	SIZE	STU#	GENDER	SCORE
1	Central High	1	11	35	1	M	95
1	Central High	1	11	35	2	M	86
1	Central High	1	11	35	3	F	97
1	Central High	2	11	32	1	F	95
1	Central High	2	11	32	2	M	93

data file, like a system file, includes both data and information about the data, including variable names, variable formats, and variable and value labels.

The term *matrix* refers to data presented in a particular geometric format. A familiar example is that of the correlation matrix, such as that presented in Table 11.4. Each data value represents the correlation between two variables and is positioned at the intersection of the row and column representing those variables. The cells running diagonally from top left to lower right are called the *diagonal* of the matrix (in a correlation matrix, as in this example, cells on the diagonal will always contain the value 1.000). The default in SPSS is to present only the lower triangle of a matrix (the diagonal and the values below it, as in Table 11.5). Note that we have not lost any information by presenting only the lower triangle, because the correlations in the upper triangle duplicate those in the lower triangle.

Table 11.4   Correlation Matrix

	V1	V2	V3	V4
V1	1.000	.406	.476	.541
V2	.406	1.000	.493	.317
V3	.476	.493	1.000	.922
V4	.541	.317	.922	1.000

Table 11.5   Lower Triangle of Correlation Matrix

	V1	V2	V3	V4
V1	1.000			
V2	.406	1.000		
V3	.476	.493	1.000	
V4	.541	.317	.922	1.000

Matrix data files in SPSS can include different types of data matrices as well as other information, such as variable means and standard deviations. To identify the meaning of each piece of data, SPSS provides two options:

1. The variable *rowtype_*

2. The subcommand **CONTENTS**

If the first option is used, the variable *rowtype_* must be included in the data set. *Rowtype_* is a string variable with an **A8** format that can hold a specified set of values that identify the type of data each record contains. The variable *rowtype_* must be named on the **VARIABLES** subcommand of the **MATRIX DATA** command and be included in each line of data. A complete list of valid values for *rowtype_* is available in the **MATRIX DATA** chapter of the *SPSS 11.0 Syntax Reference Guide* (SPSS Inc., 2001). Some of the most common are **CORR** (correlation), **COV** (covariance), **MEAN** (mean), **STDEV** (standard deviation), and **N** (count). Matrix data by default are read in **FREE** format, so values should be separated by delimiters (in this case, blanks), but column locations do not have to be specified. The following syntax reads the mean (**MEAN**), standard deviation (**STD**), count (**N**), and correlation matrix for the variables *score1*, *score2*, *score3*, and *score4* and converts this information into a matrix data file:

```
* Reading a correlation matrix using rowtype_.
MATRIX DATA VARIABLES = rowtype_ score1 TO score4.
BEGIN DATA
MEAN 3.0 3.2 3.2 2.8
STD 1.3 1.6 1.3 1.2
N 50 50 50 50
CORR 1
CORR .406 1
CORR .476 .493 1
CORR .541 .317 .922 1
END DATA.
LIST VAR = ALL.
```

Output from the **LIST** is presented in Table 11.6. The first variable in each row is *rowtype_*, which identifies what type of data is included on that row. For instance, the second row contains the means for each variable, and the last four rows contain the correlation matrix. The *varname_* variable is created by SPSS from the variable names specified with the **VARIABLES** keyword of the **MATRIX DATA** command and is used to label the rows of the correlation matrix. The matrix data file includes the full correlation matrix, although only the lower triangle was supplied in the **MATRIX DATA** command.

Table 11.6   SPSS Matrix Data Set Created From Raw Matrix Data

ROWTYPE_	VARNAME_	SCORE1	SCORE2	SCORE3	SCORE4
N		50.0000	50.0000	50.0000	50.0000
MEAN		3.0000	3.2000	3.2000	2.8000
STDDEV		1.3000	1.6000	1.3000	1.2000
CORR	SCORE1	1.0000	.4060	.4760	.5410
CORR	SCORE2	.4060	1.0000	.4930	.3170
CORR	SCORE3	.4760	.4930	1.0000	.9220
CORR	SCORE4	.5410	.3170	.9220	1.0000

If the *rowtype_* variable is not used, the **CONTENTS** subcommand must be used to specify the meaning of each row of data. The keywords that may be used with **CONTENTS** are the same as the values that may be used for *rowtype_*. The following syntax uses the **CONTENTS** subcommand to read matrix input and create a matrix data set:

```
* Reading a correlation matrix using / CONTENTS.
MATRIX DATA VARIABLES = score1 TO score4
   / CONTENTS = MEAN STD N CORR.
BEGIN DATA
3.0 3.2 3.2 2.8
1.3 1.6 1.3 1.2
50 50 50 50
1
.406 1
.476 .493 1
.541 .317 .922 1
END DATA.
LIST VAR = ALL.
```

The **CONTENTS** subcommand names the type of data found on each line of the input file. **CORR** (meaning *correlation*) does not have to be repeated four times: The fact that four variables (*score1* to *score4*) are specified with the **VARIABLES** keyword tells SPSS that the correlation matrix will have four lines. The output from the **LIST** command will be identical to that presented in Table 11.6.

A matrix data file created using either method can be used as input to a number of SPSS commands. The syntax below uses the matrix data file created above as input to the SPSS **RELIABILITY** procedure:

```
* Computing reliability with matrix input.
RELIABILITY VARIABLES = score1 to score4
   / SCALE (scores) = score1 to score4
   / MATRIX = IN(*)
   / MODEL = ALPHA.
```

The subcommand **/ MATRIX = IN(*)** tells SPSS that the data to be analyzed are in matrix format and that they represent the current active file. This is provided as an example of a command using matrix input. Discussion of the **RELIABILITY** command is beyond the scope of this book. If you do run this command, you will get the results presented in Table 11.7.

Table 11.7   Results of Reliability Analysis Performed With Matrix Input

RELIABILITY ANALYSIS — SCALE (SCORES)

N of Cases =	50.0
Reliability Coefficients	4 items
Alpha = .8017	Standardized item alpha = .8160

⠿ CHAPTER 12

Saving Data Files

This chapter discusses saving data files in different formats. Topics include

○ Saving SPSS system and portable files

○ Saving files for use by database or spreadsheet programs

○ Saving text files

SPSS has the capacity to save data files (also knows as *writing files*) in a number of formats. If the data will be used in SPSS, they should be saved as a system file or portable file. If they will be used by another program, in some cases they may be saved in a format specific to that program, and if not, they may be saved as a text file or tab-delimited file. Information about the different types of files is also found in Chapters 8 (text files), 9 (SPSS system and portable files), and 10 (files created by other programs).

SAVING AN SPSS SYSTEM FILE

SPSS system files are saved with the **SAVE** or **XSAVE** commands. The **SAVE** command is executed immediately, whereas **XSAVE** is not executed until an **EXECUTE** command is reached or a subsequent command causes the data to be read. This reduces processing time by accomplishing two tasks in one data pass. The basic command to save a system file is,

```
SAVE OUTFILE = newfile.
```

or

```
XSAVE OUTFILE = newfile.
```

Either command will save the active file, excluding scratch variables, as a system file at the location associated with the alias *newfile* (aliases are discussed in Chapter 8). The **RENAME, DROP, KEEP,** and **MAP** subcommands are available with **SAVE** and **XSAVE**, as they are with the **GET FILE** command discussed in Chapter 9.

SAVING AN SPSS PORTABLE DATA FILE

SPSS portable data files are used to share data among programmers using SPSS under different operating systems when a system file cannot be shared by the two systems. They consist of 80-character records, so longer records must be spread over several lines. Portable data files are produced with the **EXPORT** command. The subcommands **DROP, KEEP, RENAME,** and **MAP** are available with **EXPORT**, as they are with the **GET FILE** command discussed in Chapter 9. The following command will save a portable file named *port1*, which contains the variables *id, var1, var2,* and *var3:*

```
EXPORT OUTFILE = port1
   / KEEP = id var1 var2 var3 var3.
```

SAVING A DATA FILE FOR USE BY OTHER PROGRAMS

The **SAVE TRANSLATE** command can save the active file in formats specific to several spreadsheet and database programs, such as Microsoft Excel, and to write data to a database through the use of ODBC (Open DataBase Connectivity) if you have the necessary drivers. A complete list of the supported programs and the specific requirements and limitations of each can be found in the *SPSS 11.0 Syntax Reference Guide* (SPSS Inc., 2001), in the chapter on the **SAVE TRANSLATE** command.

The following syntax will save the active data file as an Excel spreadsheet and translate the variable names to field names:

```
SAVE TRANSLATE OUTFILE = newfile
   / TYPE = XLS
   / FIELDNAMES.
```

The **KEEP, DROP, RENAME,** and **MAP** subcommands are available, as they are with the **GET FILE** command discussed in Chapter 9. **SAVE**

TRANSLATE can be used to write data to a database using ODBC but requires a detailed **CONNECT** subcommand. It is recommended that you obtain the **CONNECT** syntax by opening the database file with the SPSS text wizard (choose **File**, **Open Database**, **New Query** from the menu system). The resulting syntax can be pasted to a syntax file and incorporated into the **SAVE TRANSLATE** command.

  SAVE TRANSLATE can also save a data file in tab-delimited format, a format that can be read by many other programs. The following syntax will write a tab-delimited file with the variable names written into the first row:

```
SAVE TRANSLATE OUTFILE = newfile
   / TYPE = TAB
   / FIELDNAMES.
```

SAVING TEXT FILES

The **WRITE** command produces a text file that can be read by most text processors. The distinguishing characteristic of text files, also known as *raw data files* or *ASCII files*, is that they contain only data and formats, not information such as variable labels. The following is the basic command to write all variables in the active file, with their current dictionary formats, to a new text file:

```
WRITE OUTFILE = newfile / ALL.
```

  WRITE is a transformation command, so it will not be executed unless followed by the **EXECUTE** command or another command that causes the data file to be read. You can write a subset of variables from the active file to the new file by naming them in place of the keyword **ALL**, as in the following example:

```
WRITE OUTFILE = newfile / var1 var2 var3.
```

  By default, variables are written to a text file using the write formats from the active file and without spaces between variables, but these defaults can be overridden by the **WRITE** command. The syntax below demonstrates how to specify column locations in the new text file:

```
WRITE OUTFILE = text1 / v1 1-2 v2 4-5 v3 7-8.
```

Spaces can also be specified by including them as literals in the **WRITE** command, as in the following example:

```
WRITE OUTFILE = text1 /v1 ` ` v2 ` ` v3 ` `.
```

The same technique can be used to write text strings into the new file: Any text enclosed between quotation marks or apostrophes will be written into each new record.

Formats for numeric variables can be changed in the **WRITE** command. This is demonstrated in the following syntax:

```
WRITE OUTFILE = text1 / v1 v2 v3 (3F2.0).
```

The variables *v1*, *v2*, and *v3* will be written to the text file *text1* with the format **F2.0**.

The **TABLE** keyword creates a table showing the names, locations, and formats of variables in the new file. It is demonstrated in the following syntax:

```
WRITE OUTFILE = text TABLE / v1 v2 v3 (3F2.0).
```

Output from the **TABLE** subcommand is similar to that presented in Table 12.1.

Table 12.1   Variable Table Created With the **WRITE OUTFILE** Command

Variable	Rec	Start	End	Format
V1	1	1	2	F2.0
V2	1	3	4	F2.0
V3	1	5	6	F2.0

Part IV

File Manipulation and Management in SPSS

CHAPTER 13

Inspecting a Data File

This chapter discusses ways to get basic information about a data file. Topics include

○ Determining the number of cases in a file

○ Determining what variables are in a file

○ Getting information about the variables in the file

○ Checking for duplicate cases

○ Looking at variable values and distributions

○ Creating standardized scores

Often, a statistician is simply presented with a data file and expected to begin working with it. In this situation, you must familiarize yourself with the file and its contents before beginning the analysis. You can draw on two basic sources of information:

1. *The owners of the data.* This means the people in charge of the project that produced the data and, by extension, the people who worked on the project. They should supply you with information such as the purpose of the project, when and how the data were collected, and what cleaning procedures have been done on the file. If you are fortunate, written documentation will be available, including a codebook identifying variables and coding schemes, and a copy of any instruments that were used to collect data.

2. *The data file itself.* Even if a project is copiously documented, you have to verify that the file you received matches the documentation. In particular, you need to check the file for obvious errors and get

a sense of the distributions of the variables and the amount and distribution of missing data.

The processes described in Point #2 are sometimes referred to as *data screening* because they represent a preliminary look at the data file. Often, the data-screening process will discover problems such as out-of-range values or duplicate records, which will require consultation with the owners of the data. As preparation for such discussions, it is wise to produce a basic report on the file and its contents, including the type of information gained from the procedures discussed in this chapter. Data screening is a complex topic covered in greater depth in books such as *Using Multivariate Statistics* (Tabachnick & Fidell, 2001).

DETERMINING THE NUMBER OF CASES IN A FILE

The command,

```
SHOW N.
```

will produce output that displays the unweighted number of cases in the working data file, for instance, N = 1,104. This information helps to confirm that you were given the correct file and that no cases were lost in transport.

DETERMINING WHAT VARIABLES ARE IN A FILE

You can produce a list of variable names with the **DISPLAY** command and paste the output into a word-processing file. This is useful because you can then use the **Find** procedure within the word-processing program to search for variables by name. The **DISPLAY** command is demonstrated in the following syntax:

```
* What variables are in the file?.
DATA LIST / first second third fourth fifth 1-5.
BEGIN DATA
12345
END DATA.
DISPLAY NAMES.
DISPLAY SORTED NAMES.
```

DISPLAY NAMES lists the variable names in file order, as in Table 13.1, and **DISPLAY SORTED NAMES** lists the variable names in alphabetical order, as in Table 13.2.

Table 13.1   Variable Names in File Order

Currently Defined Variables

FIRST	SECOND	THIRD	FOURTH	FIFTH

Table 13.2   Variable Names in Alphabetical Order

Currently Defined Variables

FIFTH	FIRST	FOURTH	SECOND	THIRD

GETTING MORE INFORMATION ABOUT THE VARIABLES

The command **DISPLAY DICTIONARY** will display the complete data dictionary. By default, the dictionary for the entire active file is displayed, but you can also request information for specific variables only. The command,

```
DISPLAY DICTIONARY
     / VAR = standard.
```

will produce output similar to that in Table 13.3. This table gives us the following information for the hypothetical variable *standard:*

1. It has the variable label "Meets some exercise standard."

2. It begins in Column 310.

3. It has a width of 2, so it occupies Columns 310 and 311.

4. It is right aligned.

5. It has two labeled values: 0 is labeled "Yes" and 1 is labeled "No."

6. 99 is defined as a missing value.

7. It uses the print and write formats F2.0.

Table 13.3   Dictionary Information for the Variable *standard*

Name		Position
STANDARD	Meets some exercise standard Measurement Level: Scale Column Width: 2 Alignment: Right Print Format: F2.0 Write Format: F2.0 Missing Values: 99	310

	Value	Label
	0	No
	1	Yes

CHECKING FOR DUPLICATE CASES

In many data files, each case has a *unique identifier*. This is a variable or combination of variables that has a *unique* value for each case and can be used to *identify* a particular case. If a data file has a unique identifier, you need to confirm that it is in fact unique, in other words, that there are no duplicate values on that variable. The easiest way to do this is to produce a frequency table for the identifier, sorted on descending frequency (specified with the keyword **DFREQ**) so the most frequent case appears first in the table. The syntax below will produce such a table for the variable *id:*

```
FREQ VAR = id / FORMAT = DFREQ.
```

If a supposedly unique identifier appears more than once in your file, you need to determine why. Looking at the values of other variables for the cases with duplicate identifiers may help you decide whether cases are duplicates or whether they are different cases mistakenly assigned the same identifier. The following code will list the values for all variables for the cases with the value '05732' on the string variable *id:*

```
TEMP.
SELECT IF id = '05732'.
LIST VARIABLES = ALL.
```

The **TEMP** (**TEMPORARY**) command is important, because it makes the selection that follows temporary. If it is omitted, the selection will be permanent and the only cases left in the active file will be those with the value '05732' on *id*. If there are many variables in the file, you may want to list only those that will be most helpful in identifying cases, for instance,

```
TEMP.
SELECT IF ID = '05732'.
LIST VARIABLES = fname lname address bdate.
```

If you decide that the cases with duplicate *id* values are, in fact, duplicate records, there are several ways to eliminate them, as discussed in Chapter 15. This is the type of decision that normally requires consultation with the owner of the data.

You may want to count how many times values are duplicated on sets of variables within a data set, because this will give you an idea of how many potential duplicates the file contains. The following syntax will count the number of duplicates (here defined as cases with identical values on all variables in the file) and write that number into the variable *numdup:*

```
DATA LIST / v1 v2 v3 1-6.
BEGIN DATA
1 2 3
1 2 3
1 2 3
1 2 2
1 3 3
END DATA.
AGGREGATE OUTFILE = *
    / BREAK = ALL
    / numdup = N.
LIST VAR = ALL.
```

Output from the **LIST** command is displayed in Table 13.4. Any value greater than 1 on the variable *numdup* indicates sets of records with identical values. In this file, there are three records with identical values on all variables.

Table 13.4 Data Set With Count of Duplicate Cases

V1	V2	V3	NUMDUP
1	2	2	1
1	2	3	3
1	3	3	1

LOOKING AT VARIABLE VALUES AND DISTRIBUTIONS

The easiest way to look at the values on individual variables is through the **FREQUENCIES** command, which is most appropriate for variables with only a few values. The **FREQUENCIES** command is demonstrated in the syntax below:

```
* Simple frequencies command.
DATA LIST FREE / var1.
BEGIN DATA
1 2 1 3 2 3
END DATA.
FORMAT var1 (F1.0).
FREQ VAR = var1.
```

Output from the **FREQUENCIES** command is presented in Tables 13.5 and 13.6. Table 13.5 displays the number of valid and missing values for *var1*, and in this case there are six valid values and no missing values. Table 13.6 displays the values for *var1*, their frequencies, and what percentage each value represents of total and valid (non-missing) cases.

Table 13.5 Summary Table Produced With **FREQUENCIES** Command

N		
	Valid	6
	Missing	0

The **FREQUENCIES** command can also produce statistics and graphical displays. The following syntax suppresses the frequency table with the subcommand **FORMAT = NOTABLE** and requests a barchart and the mean, standard deviation, skewness, and standard error of skewness for the hypothetical variable *age:*

Table 13.6   Frequency Table Produced With **FREQUENCIES** Command

		Frequency	Percent	Valid Percent	Cumulative Percent
Valid	1	2	33.3	33.3	33.3
	2	2	33.3	33.3	66.7
	3	2	33.3	33.3	100.0
	Total	6	100.0	100.0	

```
FREQ VAR = age / FORMAT = NOTABLE
    / BARCHART
    / STATS = MEAN STDDEV SKEW SESKEW.
```

Many other statistics and charts can be produced with the **FREQUEN-CIES** command. These are discussed in the **FREQUENCIES** chapter of the *SPSS 11.0 Syntax Reference Guide* (SPSS Inc., 2001).

The **EXAMINE** command produces a number of statistics and graphics that are useful when exploring a new data file. The syntax below will produce the default output for *var1:*

```
EXAMINE VAR = var1.
```

This will include a stem-and-leaf diagram, a boxplot, and the statistics presented in Table 13.7.

Table 13.7   Statistics Produced With **EXAMINE** Command

			Statistic	Std. Error
VAR1	Mean		2.00	.365
	95% Confidence Interval for Mean	Upper Bound Lower Bound	1.06 2.94	
	5% Trimmed Mean		2.00	
	Median		2.00	
	Variance		.800	
	Std. Deviation		.894	

(Continued)

Table 13.7 (Continued)

		Statistic	Std. Error
Minimum		1	
Maximum		3	
Range		2	
Interquartile Range		2.00	
Skewness		.000	.845
Kurtosis		−1.875	1.741

CREATING STANDARDIZED SCORES

One way to screen a data set for extreme values or *outliers* is through the use of *standardized scores,* also known as *z-scores* or *normal scores.* These scores express the data values for each variable as units of that variable's standard deviation, with the value 0 representing the mean for that variable. There are no absolute rules about when a standard score is "too large," but one rule of thumb is to look closely at data with z-scores larger than 2 or 3. The use of standardized scores to screen for outliers is demonstrated in the syntax below:

```
DATA LIST FREE / id var1.
BEGIN DATA
1 1 2 1 3 2 4 33 5 2 6 2 7 3 8 3 9 3 10 1
END DATA.
DESCR VAR = var1 / SAVE.
TEMP.
SELECT IF zvar1 GT 2 OR zvar1 LT-2.
LIST VAR = ALL.
```

The **DESCR** command creates z-scores for the variables named, in this case for var1. The new variable will have the name of the source variable plus the letter z, so the z-score for *var1* is named *zvar1*. We use the z-scores thus created to select cases with extreme values, using the **SELECT** command. The **LIST** command will produce the data presented in Table 13.8; a case with a value of 33.0 from a variable with a mean of 5.1 warrants further attention, and the z-score of 2.84 also tells us this is an extreme value for the variable in question.

Table 13.8   Statistics Produced With **DESCRIPTIVES** Command

	N	Minimum	Maximum	Mean	Std. Deviation
VAR1	10	1.00	33.00	5.1000	9.83700
Valid N (listwise)	10				

The **SELECT** command selects cases with standardized scores that are more than 2 standard deviations away from the mean, that is, with scores on *zvar1* outside the range (–2, 2). The **LIST** command displays values from these extreme cases, as presented in Table 13.9. Case 4 has the value 33 for *var1*, which translates to a z-value over 2.8, meaning it is almost 3 standard deviations higher than the mean. In fact, this value appears to be due to data entry error, because it has a value of 33 while no other case has a value higher than 3. Of course, the decision on which values should be corrected or deleted must be reached in consultation with the owners of the data.

Table 13.9   Selection of Case With Extreme Z-score

ID	VAR1	ZVAR1
4.00	33.00	2.83623

CHAPTER 14

Combining Data Files

T his chapter discusses how to combine cases or variables from several data files into one file. Topics include

- ❍ Adding new variables to existing cases
- ❍ Adding summary data to an individual-level file
- ❍ Combining cases from several files
- ❍ Updating values in a file

The first two situations are handled with the **MATCH FILES** command, the third with the **ADD FILES** command, and the fourth with the **UPDATE** command. The following points apply to all three commands:

1. All data files involved must be SPSS system files or the current active file.
2. If key variables are used, they must exist and have the same name in all files.
3. If key variables are used, the data files must be sorted in ascending order on those variables.
4. The **RENAME, DROP, KEEP**, and **MAP** subcommands are available with all three commands, as with the **GET FILE** command discussed in Chapter 9.
5. All three procedures create a new active data file.

ADDING NEW VARIABLES TO EXISTING CASES

MATCH FILES allows you to combine variables from two or more (up to 50) files. Files are usually combined in a *nonparallel* match, meaning that cases are identified by their values on one or more *key variables* specified on the **BY** subcommand. The key variables act as unique identifiers, as discussed in Chapter 13: A particular combination of key variables identifies a case and differentiates it from all other cases. The syntax below matches two files, one containing each student's age and the other, the student's grade in school:

```
* Create the first file.
DATA LIST FREE / id age.
BEGIN DATA
1 15 2 16 4 15 3 17 5 18
END DATA.
SORT CASES BY ID.
SAVE OUTFILE = data1.
* Create the second file.
DATA LIST FREE / id grade.
BEGIN DATA
1 9 2 10 4 9 3 11 5 12
END DATA.
SORT CASES BY ID.
SAVE OUTFILE = data2.
* Match the two files (nonparallel).
MATCH FILES FILE = data1
   / FILE = data2
   / BY id.
FORMATS ALL (F2.0).
LIST VAR = ALL.
```

This syntax reads two data files into SPSS, sorts each by the key variable *id*, and saves each as a system file. The **MATCH FILES** command combines these files into a new active file, matching cases by the key variable *id*. Output from the **LIST** command is displayed in Table 14.1. If the same variable name occurs in one or more of the files, the value from the file named first will appear in the combined file.

Table 14.1   Matched Data File

ID	AGE	GRADE
1	15	9
2	16	10
3	17	11
4	15	9
5	18	12

In a *parallel* match, two or more files are matched without using a key variable to identify cases, so the **BY** subcommand is not used. This technique is useful when the files have been sorted by a key variable, such as a patient identification number, and then the key variable has been removed from the files for confidentiality reasons. It is critical that the files to be combined contain the same cases in the same order, because cases are identified only by their positions in the file.

The **IN** subcommand creates an indicator variable that takes the value 1 if a case exists in a file, and 0 otherwise. This is useful because it allows you to see how many cases from each file were matched by cases in the other files. The **IN** subcommand is demonstrated in the syntax below:

```
* Using the IN subcommand with MATCH FILES.
* Create the first file.
DATA LIST FREE / id v1.
BEGIN DATA
1 1 2 2 3 3 4 4
END DATA.
SORT CASES BY id.
SAVE OUTFILE = data3.
* Create the second file.
DATA LIST FREE / id v2.
BEGIN DATA
1 5 2 6 3 7 4 8 5 9
END DATA.
SORT CASES BY id.
SAVE OUTFILE = data4.
* Match the files and check the match.
MATCH FILES FILE = data3 / IN = in3
   / FILE = data4 / IN = in4
   / BY id.
CROSSTABS in3 by in4.
```

Results from the **CROSSTABS** command are presented in Table 14.2. These files did not match perfectly: One case has a value of 0 on *in3* and 1 on *in4*, meaning it exists in the file *data4* but not in *data3*. The syntax below will identify the *id* value for the case that didn't match:

```
TEMP.
SELECT IF in3 = 0 AND in4 = 1.
LIST VAR = id.
```

This will identify Case 5 (the case with the value of 5 on *id*) as the case that didn't match.

Table 14.2   Diagnostic Cross-Tabulation Table for Matched Data File

Count		IN4	Total
		1	
IN3	0	1	1
	1	4	4
Total		5	5

ADDING SUMMARY DATA TO AN INDIVIDUAL-LEVEL FILE

Often, you have a data set in which the cases are individuals who exist in natural groupings, such as patients in different medical clinics or students in different schools. You may want to add data computed at the group level, such as average age or total number of students, to the individual-level data file. Such a file can be created in two steps: First, the group-level statistics are calculated using the **AGGREGATE** command; then, the values for those statistics are matched into the individual file. The syntax below illustrates these steps:

```
* Create the individual-level file.
DATA LIST FREE / id class grade.
BEGIN DATA
1 1 95
2 1 90
3 1 93
4 2 88
5 2 91
6 2 82
END DATA.
FORMATS id class grade (F3.0).
SORT CASES BY class.
SAVE OUTFILE = ind.
* Compute the mean grade within each class.
AGGREGATE OUTFILE = *
   / BREAK = class
   / meangrad = MEAN(grade).
SAVE OUTFILE = agg.
* Match the two files.
MATCH FILES FILE = ind
```

```
    /  TABLE  =  agg
    /  BY  class.
LIST VAR = ALL.
```

The first file *(ind)* contains data on individual students: their identification number, class, and grade. The **AGGREGATE** command calculates the mean grade within each class and saves it in the file *agg.* The **MATCH FILES** command matches the two files so each student record includes the mean grade for his or her class. This type of match is called a *table lookup* match because the group-level file operates as a *table* of values, identified by the subcommand **TABLE**, from which the program *looks up* the correct values of the group-level variables for each individual case. Output from the **LIST** command is presented in Table 14.3.

Table 14.3   Individual-Level Data File Matched With Summary Information

ID	CLASS	GRADE	MEANGRAD
1	1	95	92.67
2	1	90	92.67
3	1	93	92.67
4	2	88	87.00
5	2	91	87.00
6	2	82	87.00

COMBINING CASES FROM SEVERAL FILES

The **ADD FILES** command allows you to combine cases from multiple files (up to 50) into one SPSS file. This procedure would be useful, for instance, if a school kept records for every class in a separate file and wanted to create one file containing information about every class in the school. If the **BY** subcommand is not used, the files will be *concatenated,* meaning that all cases from the first file will appear in the combined file, followed by all cases from the second file, and so on. If the **BY** subcommand is used, the files will be *interleaved,* so cases in the combined file will be ordered by their values on the **BY** variables. The difference in these two methods is illustrated in the following syntax:

```
* Create the first file.
DATA LIST FREE / id v1.
BEGIN DATA
1 1 3 1
END DATA.
SORT CASES BY ID.
SAVE OUTFILE = add1.
* Create the second file.
DATA LIST FREE / id v1.
BEGIN DATA
2 2 4 2
END DATA.
SORT CASES BY ID.
SAVE OUTFILE = add2.
* Add files by concatenation.
ADD FILES FILE = add1
    / FILE = add2.
LIST VAR = ALL.
* Add files by interleaving.
ADD FILES FILE = add1
    / FILE = add2 / BY id.
LIST VAR = ALL.
```

Output from the first **LIST** command displays the contents of the concatenated file, as presented in Table 14.4. This file consists of the cases from the file *add1* followed by the cases from the file *add2*. Output from the second **LIST** command displays the contents of the interleaved file, as presented in Table 14.5. This file consists of the cases from both files, ordered by the value of the variable *id:* The first case comes from *add1*, the second from *add2*, and so on.

Table 14.4   Files Added by Concatenation

ID	V1
1.00	1.00
3.00	1.00
2.00	2.00
4.00	2.00

UPDATING VALUES IN A FILE

The **UPDATE** command allows you to update values in a *master* file, using data from one or more *transaction* files. The master file is named first in the command, and the master and transaction files must be linked by one or more key variables named on the **BY** subcommand.

Table 14.5   Files Added by Interleaving

ID	V1
1.00	1.00
2.00	2.00
3.00	1.00
4.00	2.00

The **UPDATE** command copies all the variables from the master file into a new active file, then copies the variables from the first transaction file into the active file, then the variables from the second transaction file, and so on. Values are updated when their cases match on the **BY** variables. The basic principle behind the **UPDATE** command is that the most recent valid value will appear in the updated file, so it is important that the transaction files be listed in the correct order (most recent last). Only valid data are used to update the active file, so missing data will never overwrite valid data. The **UPDATE** command is illustrated in the following syntax:

```
* Using the UPDATE command.
* Create the master file.
DATA LIST FREE / id v1.
BEGIN DATA
1 1
2 1
3 1
END DATA.
SORT CASES BY id.
SAVE OUTFILE = master.
* Create the first transaction file.
DATA LIST FREE / id v1.
```

```
BEGIN DATA
1 2
END DATA.
SORT CASES BY id.
SAVE OUTFILE = trans1.
* Create the second transaction file.
DATA LIST FREE / id v1.
BEGIN DATA
1 .
3 3
END DATA.
SORT CASES BY id.
SAVE OUTFILE = trans2.
UPDATE FILE = master
    / FILE = trans1
    / FILE = trans2
    / BY id.
FORMATS ALL (F1.0).
LIST VAR = ALL.
```

Output from the **LIST** command is displayed in Table 14.6. The updated file includes one case (*id* = 2) from the master file, one from the first transaction file (*id* = 1), and one from the second transaction file (*id* = 3). Note that the invalid value for Case 1 in the second transaction file did not overwrite the valid value from the first transaction file.

Table 14.6   Updated Data File

ID	V1
1	2
2	1
3	3

CHAPTER 15

Data File Management

This chapter discusses syntax for file management functions, including the following topics:

○ Reordering and dropping variables in the active file

○ Eliminating duplicate records

○ Sorting a data set

○ Splitting a data set

○ Making temporary and permanent case selections

○ Weighting cases

REORDERING AND DROPPING VARIABLES IN THE ACTIVE FILE

You can reorder or drop variables in the active file by matching the file to itself, using the **KEEP** and **DROP** subcommands to change the variable order or drop variables. These subcommands operate in the same manner as they do with the **GET FILE** command discussed in Chapter 9. The following syntax reverses the order of variables in the active file and drops one variable:

```
DATA LIST FREE / var1 var2 var3 var4 var5.
BEGIN DATA
1 2 3 4 5
6 7 8 9 10
END DATA.
```

```
MATCH FILES FILE = *
    / KEEP = var5 var4 var3 var2.
EXE.
FORMATS ALL (F2.0).
LIST VAR = ALL.
```

Output from the **LIST** command is displayed in Table 15.1.

Table 15.1   Active File With Cases Reordered and One Case
Dropped

VAR5	VAR4	VAR3	VAR2
5	4	3	2
10	9	8	7

ELIMINATING DUPLICATE RECORDS

Screening data files for duplicate records was discussed in Chapter 13. If
you have established that a file contains duplicates that should be deleted,
there are several ways to accomplish this. The syntax below demonstrates a
technique to create a new active file without duplicates, when duplicates
are defined as cases with identical values on all variables:

```
DATA LIST FREE / id var1 var2 var3.
BEGIN DATA
101  1  2  3
102  1  2  2
102  1  2  2
103  1  2  3
103  1  2  3
END DATA.
SORT CASES BY id var1 var2 var3.
MATCH FILES FILE = *
    / BY ALL
    / FIRST = first1.
FORMATS ALL (F3.0).
SELECT IF first1 = 1.
LIST VAR = ALL.
```

There are five case in the data file created by the **DATA LIST** command,
two of which are duplicates of other cases. The output from the **LIST**

command, which displays the contents of the file after the duplicate cases have been eliminated, is presented in Table 15.2.

Table 15.2   Data File With Duplicate Records Eliminated

ID	VAR1	VAR2	VAR3	FIRST1
101	1	2	3	1
102	1	2	2	1
103	1	2	3	1

The key to this technique is the creation of the variable *first1*, which has a value of 1 for the first case with a particular set of values and a value of 0 for any subsequent cases with identical values. Because the file has been sorted on all variables, cases with the same values for all variables will appear consecutively.

A different situation is presented when you have meaningful criteria that will help you decide which records to keep. For instance, you may have a file containing multiple records for individuals, with a variable indicating when a particular record was entered. You can use this variable to select and keep only the most recently entered record for each individual. The following code will retain the record for each individual, with the most recent value on *date1:*

```
* Meaningful selection from records with duplicate
  identifiers.
DATA LIST FREE / id (F3.0) date1 (DATE9) score (F3.0).
BEGIN DATA
101 1-jan-01 88
101 5-feb-01 75
101 13-apr-01 91
102 3-jan-01 93
102 4-feb-01 85
103 6-jan-01 91
END DATA.
SORT CASES BY id (A) date1 (D).
DO IF $CASENUM = 1.
COMPUTE flag = 1.
ELSE IF id = LAG(id).
COMPUTE flag = 0.
ELSE.
```

```
COMPUTE flag = 1.
END IF.
EXE.
FORMAT FLAG (F1.0).
SELECT IF flag = 1.
LIST VAR = ALL.
```

This data set has three records for *id #101*, two for *id #102*, and one for *id #103*. This syntax uses the **LAG** function to create a flag variable with the value of 1 for the first record from each group with the same value on *id*, and a value of 0 otherwise. Because the file is sorted in descending order by the date variable (*date1*), the first record in each group will be the most recent. The **SELECT** command retains records with a value of 1 on *flag*. Output from the **LIST** command is presented in Table 15.3.

Table 15.3   Data File With Most Recent Records for Each Case Retained

ID	DATE1	SCORE	FLAG
101	13-APR-01	91	1
102	04-FEB-01	85	1
103	06-JAN-01	91	1

SORTING A DATA SET

Sorting a data set is done for many reasons: It is a prerequisite to using certain procedures, such as **MATCH FILES** and **UPDATE**, and a sorted data set is easier to proofread and examine for patterns. The basic command structure is as follows:

```
SORT CASES BY var1.
```

where *var1* is the variable used to sort the active file. The keyword **BY** is optional:

```
SORT CASES var1.
```

and would produce the same result. By default, cases are sorted in ascending order (with the lowest value first). To sort in descending order (with the highest value first), add the keyword **(D)**.

You can specify several sort variables. SPSS will sort all cases on the first variable, then on the second variable within categories of the first variable, and so on. Order specifications (ascending or descending) apply to all variables to their left unless the syntax explicitly states otherwise, so if you want to sort the first variable in ascending order and the second in descending order, you must specify this, as in the syntax below:

```
SORT CASES BY var1 (A) var2 (D).
```

SPLITTING A DATA SET

The **SPLIT FILE** command makes it possible to repeat analyses on two or more subgroups within a data file. For instance, you may have a file containing data from both male and female respondents and wish to analyze the data for men and women separately. The easiest way to do this is to use the **SPLIT FILE** command, which instructs SPSS to treat the two types of cases separately without actually creating new data files. The active file must be sorted by the **SPLIT** variables, and the **SPLIT FILE** command remains in effect until it is canceled by **SPLIT FILE OFF**. The following syntax demonstrates the **SPLIT FILE** command:

```
SORT CASES BY gender.
SPLIT FILE BY gender.
REGRESSION VARS = y x1 x2 x3 x4 x5 x6
   / DEPENDENT = y
   / METHOD = ENTER.
SPLIT FILE OFF.
```

This syntax will perform the same regression analysis twice, once for men and once for women.

SELECTING CASES

The **SELECT** command selects cases according to specified logical conditions. This command should be used with caution, because by default, selections are permanent, meaning nonselected cases are removed from the active file. To do a temporary selection, precede the **SELECT** command with the **TEMPORARY** command, which specifies that the selection should apply only to the procedure immediately following. The following syntax demonstrates temporary selection:

```
TEMP.
SELECT IF (gender = 'M').
CROSSTABS race BY educ.
CROSSTABS race BY educ.
```

The first **CROSSTABS** command will include males only, while the second will include all cases.

FILTERING CASES

The **FILTER** command provides another way to select cases according to their value on some variable. It is less flexible than the **SELECT** command but has the advantage of not deleting cases from the active file. Only one filter variable may be used, and it must be numeric. The **FILTER** command excludes cases that have a value of 0 or are missing on the filter variable, so potential filter variables must be coded with this system of selection in mind. For instance, if *gender* is coded so 1 = male and 0 = female, the **FILTER** command can be used to run procedures on male cases only. This is demonstrated in the following syntax:

```
* Using a filter variable.
DATA LIST FREE / gender v2.
BEGIN DATA
1 1
1 2
1 3
0 4
0 5
END DATA.
value labels gender 1 'Male' 0 'Female'.
FILTER BY gender.
FORMATS ALL (F1.0).
LIST VAR = ALL.
FILTER OFF.
```

Output from the **LIST** command, which includes data for males (*gender* = 1) only, is presented in Table 15.4. **FILTER** does not actually remove the unselected cases from the data file, so when the **FILTER** command is canceled by **FILTER OFF**, all cases are available for analysis again.

Table 15.4   Output From Data Set Filtered by *gender*

GENDER	V2
1	1
1	2
1	3

WEIGHTING CASES

Typically, cases in a data file are *unweighted,* meaning that one case in the data file counts as one case for analytical purposes. In an unweighted data file with 30 cases, you will have an *n* of 30 for analysis, assuming no data are missing. However, sometimes data sets are meant to be *weighted* before analysis. For example, Chapter 8 includes a technique to perform a chi-square analysis by applying weights to each cell of a 2×2 table. A data file that includes weighting variables may have those weights applied or not applied. To see whether weights are currently applied to a data set, use the command,

```
SHOW WEIGHT.
```

To remove weights, use the command,

```
WEIGHT OFF.
```

To apply a weight variable, use the command,

```
WEIGHT BY wtvar.
```

where *wtvar* is the name of the variable containing the weight you want to apply.

CHAPTER 16

Restructuring Files

This chapter discusses file structure and how to change it using SPSS. Topics include

○ The unit of analysis

○ Changing file structure from univariate to multivariate

○ Including a test condition when restructuring a file

○ Changing file structure from multivariate to univariate

○ Transposing the rows and columns of a data set

THE UNIT OF ANALYSIS

The term *unit of analysis* refers to what is considered a case in a given study. For instance, in the field of education, you might be studying the performance of individual students, or you might be studying the performance of different schools. If you were studying the performance of individual students, the unit of analysis would be the *individual* and each student would be considered a case. If you were studying the average performance in different schools, the unit of analysis would be the *group* and each school would be considered a case. Most analyses are conducted at a single level of analysis, although it is possible to combine data from different levels into one model. This type of analysis requires multilevel modeling techniques, which are beyond the scope of this book. A standard reference on multilevel modeling is *Hierarchical Linear Models* (Raudenbush & Bryk, 2002).

Unit of analysis is also relevant to studies that collect data on more than one occasion from the same individuals. For instance, lab rats could be weighed weekly to see whether they are gaining weight, or students could be tested monthly to see whether their vocabulary size is increasing. In this type of study, the unit of analysis may be either the occasion of measurement or the individual from whom repeated measurements are taken.

A *univariate* file structure is organized so that each line of the file contains data from one occasion of measurement for one individual. For instance, a univariate file containing student grades collected at three time points would have three lines of data for each student. This arrangement is typical when the unit of analysis is the occasion of measurement. The same data could also be arranged in a file so all data pertaining to a student appears on a single line. This is *multivariate* structure and is typically used when the unit of analysis is the individual and occasions of measurement are considered repeated measurements within each individual. The difference is demonstrated in Tables 16.1 and 16.2 below.

Table 16.1　Univariate Data File

ID	TIME	SCORE
1	1	93
1	2	85
1	3	89
2	1	88
2	2	90
2	3	81

Table 16.2　Multivariate Data File

ID	SCORE1	SCORE2	SCORE3
1	93	85	89
2	88	90	81

CHANGING FILE STRUCTURE FROM UNIVARIATE TO MULTIVARIATE

Changing a file's structure from univariate to multivariate is sometimes referred to as changing a file from *narrow* to *wide*, or from *simple* to *complex*. The following syntax restructures a univariate file as multivariate:

```
* Restructuring a univariate file as multivariate.
DATA LIST / student 1 time 3 score 5-7.
BEGIN DATA
1 1 90
1 2 81
1 3 82
2 1 79
2 3 98
3 1 91
3 2 95
3 3 93
END DATA.
SORT CASES by student.
LIST VAR = ALL.
CASESTOVARS
    / ID = student
    / INDEX = time.
LIST VAR = ALL.
```

The **CASESTOVAR** command performs the file restructuring. As the name implies, repeated measurements that were treated as *cases* in the original file become *variables* in the new file. The subcommand **ID** indicates the variable that defines a case in the multivariate file *(student)*, and the subcommand **INDEX** indicates the variable that identifies an occasion of measurement *(time)*. Output from the first **LIST** command is displayed in Table 16.3, which displays the structure of the univariate file: Each line contains the data from one occasion of measurement for one person. Output from the second **LIST** command is displayed in Table 16.4, which displays the structure of the multivariate file created by the **CASESTOVARS** command: Each line contains the data from all occasions of measurement for one person. Note that new variable names have been created for each occasion of measurement: *score.1*, *score.2*, and *score.3*. These names were created by SPSS using two pieces of information:

1. The stem from the name of the variable representing the measurement *(score)*.

2. The suffix *(.1, .2, or .3)* representing the occasion of measurement, as taken from the variable *time*.

Table 16.3   Univariate Data File

ID	TIME	SCORE
1	1	90
1	2	81
1	3	82
2	1	79
2	3	98
3	1	91
3	2	95
3	3	93

Table 16.4   Univariate File (Table 16.3) Restructured as Multivariate

ID	SCORE1	SCORE2	SCORE3
1	90	81	82
2	79	.	98
3	91	95	93

CASESTOVARS assumes that each case in the multivariate file should have the same occasions of measurement. In this example, the second case did not have a score for time 2, but SPSS still created the variable *score.2* for that case and assigned it the system-missing value.

Another way to restructure files from univariate to multivariate is to use the **VECTOR**, **DO REPEAT**, and **AGGREGATE** commands, which are further discussed in Chapter 25. This technique is demonstrated in the syntax below, which performs the same file restructuring as the **CASESTOVARS** command did in the program above:

```
* Using vectors to restructure a univariate file as
multivariate.
DATA LIST / student 1 time 3 score_ 5-7.
BEGIN DATA
1 1 90
1 2 81
1 3 82
2 1 79
2 3 98
3 1 91
3 2 95
```

```
3 3 93
END DATA.
* Create new variables.
VECTOR score_ (3F2.0).
* Write the values into these variables.
DO REPEAT a = score_ / b = score_.
COMPUTE a(time) = b.
END REPEAT.
EXE.
LIST VARS = ALL.
* Aggregate file so only valid values are retained.
AGGREGATE OUTFILE = *
    / BREAK = student
    / score_1 TO score_3 = MAX(score_1 to score_3).
LIST VAR = ALL.
```

The **VECTOR** command creates three **F2.0** variables, named *score_1*, *score_2*, and *score_3*. The **DO REPEAT–END REPEAT** command structure writes the values from each occasion of *score* to the respective *score_* variable. For instance, the scores for time 1 are written to the variable *score_1*. Output from the first **LIST** command, which represents the data file after the execution of the **DO REPEAT–END REPEAT** structure, is presented in Table 16.5. Each line of this file has a valid value for only one of the newly created variables *score_1*, *score_2*, and *score_3*. We use this fact in conjunction with the **MAX(score_1 to score_3)** function to retain only the valid values. The **MAX** function selects the largest or maximum of its arguments, and because valid values are larger than missing values, the single valid value will be selected for each case. Output from the second **LIST** command is displayed in Table 16.6, which is identical to Table 16.4 except for the variable names (e.g., SCORE.1 in Table 16.4 is SCORE_1 in Table 16.6).

Table 16.5   Data File Before Aggregation

ID	TIME	SCORE	SCORE_1	SCORE_2	SCORE_3
1	1	90	90	.	.
1	2	81	.	81	.
1	3	82	.	.	82
2	1	79	79	.	.
2	3	98	.	.	98
3	1	91	91	.	.
3	2	95	.	95	.
3	3	93	.	.	93

Table 16.6   Data File (Table 16.5) After Aggregation

ID	SCORE_1	SCORE_2	SCORE_3
1	90	81	82
2	79	.	98
3	91	95	93

INCORPORATING A TEST CONDITION WHEN RESTRUCTURING A DATA FILE

Another way to restructure a file is to apply some test condition to determine whether multiple lines of data constitute one case or several. Suppose you have a file of insurance claims for hospitalizations. In this file, a line of data contains the information for one uninterrupted stay in the hospital by one person. Each person is identified by a unique value on the variable *id*. You need to group these claims into "episodes of care," which are defined as all claims by one individual that take place without 90 or more days passing between the end of one claim and the beginning of the next. In this example, the case is one "episode of care." The following syntax accomplishes this restructuring:

```
* Restructuring a data file using the LAG function.
* Test condition: new episode = gap of more than 90
  days between claims.
DATA LIST / id 1 start 3-12 (date) end 15-24 (date).
BEGIN DATA
1 11-JAN-90    13-JAN-90
1 15-FEB-90    25-FEB-90
1 1-AUG-91     8-AUG-91
2 5-JUN-90     7-JUN-90
2 1-JUL-90     5-JUL-90
END DATA.
* Count the number of days within each claim.
COMPUTE DAYS = CTIME.DAYS(end - start).
SORT CASES BY id start.
* Assign all cases the value 1 for episode to begin
  with.
COMPUTE episode = 1.
DO IF ($CASENUM NE 1).
* Increment values of episode where appropriate.
IF id = LAG(id) and CTIME.DAYS(start-LAG(end)) LE 90
   episode = LAG(episode).
```

```
IF id = LAG(id) and CTIME.DAYS(start-LAG(end)) GT 90
   episode = LAG(episode) + 1.
END IF.
FORMAT days episode (F3.0).
* Look at the file before restructuring.
LIST VAR = ALL.
* Aggregate the file so an episode of care = a case.
AGGR OUTILE = *
   / BREAK = id episode
   / start = MIN(start)
   / end = MAX(end)
   / days = sum(days).
FORMAT days (F3.0).
* Look at the restructured file.
LIST VAR = ALL.
```

The file has been sorted by *id* and *start,* so the claims for each individual are arranged in chronological order. Output from the first **LIST** command, displayed in Table 16.7, shows the content of the unstructured file after the *days* and *episode* variables have been created. The *days* variable represents the number of days between the start and end dates in each claim. The *episode* variable is created with the **LAG** function, using the following rules:

1. Assign the value of 1 to all cases for the variable *episode.*

2. Leave this value for the first case, which is the first episode for that individual.

3. For each subsequent case, see whether the *id* variable has the same value as the previous case.
   a. If the *id* values are different, the cases represent different people, so leave the value of *episode* as it is.
   b. If the *id* values are the same, test to see how many days have elapsed between the start of the current claim and the end of the previous claim.
      i. If 90 days or fewer have elapsed, both cases belong to the same episode, so give the current case the same value of *episode* as the previous case.
      ii. If more than 90 days have elapsed, the current case belongs to a new episode, so give the current case a value of *episode* that is the value of *episode* from the previous case plus one.

Table 16.7   Univariate Data File

ID	START	END	DAYS	EPISODE
1	11-JAN-90	13-JAN-90	2	1
1	15-FEB-90	25-FEB-90	10	1
1	01-AUG-91	08-AUG-91	7	2
2	05-JUN-90	07-JUN-90	2	1
2	01-JUL-90	05-JUL-90	4	1

It can be seen from this table that *id #1* has three claims and the first two belong to the same episode, while the third belongs to a new episode. This is because only 33 days elapsed between the end of the first claim and the start of the second claim (**13-JAN-90** to **15-FEB-90**), but 522 days elapsed between the end of the second claim and the start of the third claim (**25-FEB-90** to **01-AUG-91**). Both claims for *id #2* belong to the same episode because only 24 days elapsed between the end of the first claim and the start of the second (**07-JUN-90** to **01-JUL-90**).

The final step is to restructure the file so each line of data represents one episode of care and includes the start and end dates of the episode and the total number of hospital days claimed within the episode. This is accomplished by the **AGGREGATE** command, which creates one line of data for each unique combination of *id* and *episode* and computes the following variables:

1. *days*, which is the sum of claim days within the episode

2. *start*, which is the first (**MIN**, i.e., minimum) start date of the claims within the episode

3. *end*, which is the last (**MAX**, i.e., maximum) end dates within the episode

Output of the final **LIST** command, which displays the contents of the restructured file, is presented in Table 16.8. The first and second claims from the original file were combined into one episode, with 12 total days (2 days from the first claim and 10 days from the second claim). The start date is that of the first claim, and the end date is that of the second claim. Similarly, the fourth and fifth claims were combined into one episode.

Table 16.8   Univariate File (Table 16.7) Restructured as Multivariate

ID	EPISODE	START	END	DAYS
1	1	11-JAN-90	25-FEB-90	12
1	2	01-AUG-91	08-AUG-91	7
2	1	05-JUN-90	05-JUL-90	6

CHANGING FILE STRUCTURE
FROM MULTIVARIATE TO UNIVARIATE

File structure can be changed from multivariate to univariate with the **VARSTOCASES** command, which, as the name implies, takes *variables* and makes them into *cases*. The syntax below takes the multivariate version of the data set created with the **CASESTOVARS** command above and restructures it as univariate, using the **VARSTOCASES** command:

```
* Restructuring a multivariate file as univariate.
DATA LIST / id 1 score1 2-4 score2 5-7 score3 8-10.
BEGIN DATA
1 90 81 82
2 79 . 98
3 91 95 93
END DATA.
LIST VAR = ALL.
VARSTOCASES
    / MAKE score FROM score1 to score3
    / INDEX = time.
LIST VAR = ALL.
```

The **VARSTOCASES** command performs the restructuring. The subcommand **MAKE score FROM score1 to score3** creates the variable *score* from the three variables *score1, score2,* and *score3*. The subcommand **INDEX = time** tells SPSS to create a new variable named *time* to identify the occasion of measurement. When *score* represents the value of *score1, time* equals 1; when *score* represents the value of *score2, time* equals 2, and so on. Output from the first **LIST** will be identical to that presented in Table 16.4 and displays the structure of the multivariate file. Output from the second **LIST** command will be identical to that presented in Table 16.3 and displays the structure of the univariate file.

TRANSPOSING THE ROWS AND COLUMNS OF A DATA SET

Transposing rows and columns, also known as "flipping" a data set, does not change the unit of analysis. Instead, it changes the physical format of the file so it can be analyzed by SPSS. Spreadsheets are often arranged so the rows represent variables and the columns represent cases. If you are given such a file and need to work with it in SPSS, you must transpose it so that rows represent cases and columns represent variables. This may be accomplished with the **FLIP** command, as demonstrated in the syntax below:

```
* Transposing cases and rows.
DATA LIST / case1 case2 case3 1-6.
BEGIN DATA
1 2 3
4 5 6
END DATA.
LIST VAR = ALL.
FLIP VAR = ALL.
LIST VAR = ALL.
```

Output from the first **LIST**, which displays the file as produced by the **DATA LIST** command, is displayed in Table 16.9. Output from the second **LIST** command, which displays the file after it has been flipped, is presented in Table 16.10. Note that

1. SPSS has created a new variable, *case-lbl,* which contains the variable names (*case1* to *case3*) from the original file.

2. The columns or variables have been assigned the default names *var001* and *var001.*

3. The data values have the default format **F8.2** rather than their original **F2.0** format.

Table 16.9   Data File Before Transposition

CASE1	CASE2	CASE3
1	2	3
4	5	6

Table 16.10   Data File (Table 16.9) After Transposition

CASE-LBL	VAR001	VAR002
CASE1	1.00	4.00
CASE2	2.00	5.00
CASE3	3.00	6.00

If the spreadsheet has variable names, you can retain them with the **NEWNAMES** subcommand, as demonstrated in the following syntax:

```
* Transposing cases and rows.
DATA LIST / labels 1-2 (a) case1 case2 case3 4-9.
BEGIN DATA
q1 1 2 3
q2 4 5 6
END DATA.
LIST VAR = ALL.
* Retaining variable names.
FLIP VAR = ALL
    / NEWNAMES = labels.
LIST VAR = ALL.
```

Output from the first **LIST** command, which displays the data as they were read by the **DATA LIST** command, is presented in Table 16.11. Output from the second **LIST** command, which displays the data after they have been flipped, is presented in Table 16.12. Note that in Table 16.12, the values of the variable *labels (q1* and *q2)* have been used as variable names in place of the default names *(var001* and *var002).*

Table 16.11   Data File Including the Variable *labels*

LABELS	CASE1	CASE2	CASE3
Q1	1	2	3
Q2	4	5	6

Table 16.12   Transposed Data (Table 16.11) Using *labels* as Variable Names

CASE-LBL	Q1	Q2
CASE1	1.00	4.00
CASE2	2.00	5.00
CASE3	3.00	6.00

CHAPTER 17

Missing Data in SPSS

This chapter discusses different types of missing data, how missing data is handled in SPSS, and some choices you have when dealing with missing data. Topics include the following:

○ Types of missing data

○ System-missing and user-missing data

○ Looking at patterns of missing data in a data file

○ Changing the values of blanks in numeric fields

○ Treatment of missing values in SPSS commands

○ Substituting values for missing data

The effect of missing data on arithmetic operations and functions is discussed in Chapter 22, as is a technique to control whether a function will execute when some of its arguments are missing.

Missing data is a fact of life for most data managers and analysts. The data set that contains valid values for every variable and every case is the exception rather than the rule. This chapter will not go into the theoretical issues behind the treatment of missing data, which are ably handled in *Statistical Analysis With Missing Data* (Little & Rubin, 2002). Instead, we will concentrate on how SPSS treats missing data, how you can use SPSS to examine the pattern of missing data within a file, and different approaches to dealing with missing data.

SPSS produces a module called Missing Value Analysis (MVA), which is specifically designed to display patterns of missing data in a file and to substitute values for missing data using the Expectation Maximization (EM) algorithm. This chapter assumes you do not have the MVA module. If you do, you probably would use it in preference to most of the procedures described in this chapter. However, if you don't have MVA, you can accomplish many of the same purposes using commands available in Base SPSS. One thing you cannot do in SPSS without MVA is EM estimation, so if that feature is critical to your analysis, you will have to purchase the MVA module or use another program that has this capability.

TYPES OF MISSING DATA

Several different types of data can be considered to be "missing" in a data set. First and most obvious is the case in which no data were recorded. This type of missing data will appear as blank cells or periods (.) in the data table. A second case is when you have some information, but not the information you sought. For instance, someone might decline to answer a question on a survey, and you could record that fact with a code to indicate that the question was declined, not skipped by accident. A third case is when data are missing because a question does not apply to a particular individual or group. For instance, you would not ask men whether they intended to get a mammogram in the next 12 months. You could use a code to indicate that the question was not applicable to those individuals. A fourth case is when recorded data values appear to be incorrect, for instance, if a person's age was recorded as 350 years. This is the most complicated case, because with continuous variables, there is often no clear cutoff point between valid and invalid values, and setting an acceptable range of values is partly a matter of judgment.

SYSTEM-MISSING AND USER-MISSING DATA

SPSS recognizes two types of missing data, *system-missing* and *user-missing*. The system-missing category exists only for numeric variables and is automatically applied by SPSS to invalid values, including blanks, values containing a nonnumeric character, and the values created as the result of an illegal transformation such as division by zero. String variables cannot be system-missing, because any character, including a blank, is legal in a string variable. Values assigned the system-missing value appear in the data window as periods (.) or as whatever symbol is used for the decimal point, unless this is changed by the **SET** command, as discussed below.

Both numeric and short string variables may have *user-missing* values, but long string variables cannot (the distinction between long and short string variables is discussed in Chapter 19). User-missing values are specified by the programmer. The following syntax declares the value 9 as user-missing for *var1:*

```
* Declaring user-missing values.
DATA LIST FREE / var1.
BEGIN DATA
1 1 9 2 1 2 9 2
END DATA.
MISSING VALUES var1 (9).
FORMATS var1 (F1.0).
FREQ VAR = var1.
```

Output from the **FREQ** is presented in Table 17.1, which demonstrates how SPSS reports missing values:

1. Frequency counts for valid and missing values are reported separately.

2. The "Percent" column includes both valid and missing values, while the "Valid Percent" and "Cumulative Percent" columns include only valid values.

For instance, the value 1 appears in 37.5% of the total cases but 50.0% of the valid cases.

Table 17.1   Frequency Table With User-Missing Values

			VAR1		
		Frequency	Valid Percent	Cumulative Percent	Percent
Valid	1	3	37.5	50.0	50.0
	2	3	37.5	50.0	100.0
	Total	6	75.0	100.0	
Missing	9	2	25.0		
Total		8	100.0		

Several rules apply to missing-value declarations:

1. Missing values for string variables must be enclosed in apostrophes or quotation marks.

2. Up to three missing values may be declared for each variable.

3. Different missing values for different variables may be declared on the same **MISSING VALUES** command, for instance:

```
MISSING VALUES v1 (7) v2 (8,9).
```

4. A range of values may be coded as missing, using the keywords **LO** or **LOWEST**, **THRU**, and **HI** or **HIGHEST**. For instance, the following syntax will code any value lower than 18 on *age* as missing:

```
MISSING VALUES age (LO THRU 17.99).
```

LOOKING AT MISSING DATA ON INDIVIDUAL VARIABLES

Before making any decisions about how to deal with missing data, you need to know how much data is missing on each variable and the patterns of missing data among variables. For instance, if a person is missing on *var1*, are they also likely to be missing on *var2*? How many cases are complete? How many are missing on more than two variables?

You can display the amount of missing data on individual variables using the **FREQUENCIES** command, as demonstrated in the following syntax:

```
DATA LIST FREE / var1.
BEGIN DATA
1 0 0 9 . 9 1 1
END DATA.
MISSING VALUES var1 (9).
FREQ VAR = var1 / FORMAT = NOTABLE.
```

Because these are *freefield data,* which use the blank space as a delimiter, a system-missing value must be represented by some value, in this case, a period (.). The **NOTABLE** ("no table") option suppresses the frequency table so that only the summary table presented in Table 17.2 is produced.

Table 17.2   Summary Table With Missing Data

		VAR1
N	Valid	5
	Missing	3

The following table combines user-missing and system-missing frequencies. If you want to see them separately, drop the **FORMAT = NOTABLE** subcommand and SPSS will produce the output presented in Table 17.2 plus a frequency table similar to that displayed in Table 17.3.

Table 17.3   Frequency Table With User-Missing and System-Missing Values

		Frequency	Percent	Valid Percent	Cumulative Percent
Valid	.00	2	25.0	40.0	40.0
	1.00	3	37.5	60.0	100.0
	Total	5	62.5	100.0	
Missing	9.00	2	25.0		
	System	1	12.5		
	Total	3	37.5		
Total		8	100.0		

LOOKING AT THE PATTERN OF USER-MISSING DATA AMONG PAIRS OF VARIABLES

The **CROSSTABS** command can be used to produce a table displaying the distribution of valid and user-missing values among pairs of variables. This requires using **CROSSTABS** in integer mode, specifying the range of values for each variable, and using the **MISSING = REPORT** subcommand. System-missing values cannot be displayed with the **CROSSTABS** command. The following syntax demonstrates this technique:

```
* Crosstabs to examine patterns in user-missing data.
DATA LIST FREE / var1 var2.
BEGIN DATA
1 1 1 9 2 1 9 2 9 1 9 1 9 1 1 9
1 2 1 9 9 1 1 9 9 2 2 1 1 1
END DATA.
MISSING VALUES var1 var2 (9).
* Use CROSSTABS in integer mode.
CROSSTABS VAR = var1 (1,9) var2 (1,9)
    / TABLES = var1 BY var2
    / MISSING = REPORT.
```

Output from the **CROSSTABS** command is presented in Table 17.4. The numbers in the cells represent the frequency for each combination of values, so we can see that two cases have the value of 1 on both *var1* and *var2*. Cases with missing data are reported but not included in the marginal totals. For instance, only three cases are reported as having the value 1 on *var1*, because the four cases that have the value of 1 on *var1* but are missing on *var2* are excluded from the total. We can see several interesting patterns even in this small data set. First of all, no cases are missing on both variables. Second, missing values on *var2* occur only in cases that have the value 1 on *var1*. Finally, missing data on *var1* is about equally likely to occur in cases with either value of *var2*.

Table 17.4   Cross-Tabulation Table Including User-Missing Values

		VAR2			
		1.00	2.00	9.00 (Missing)	Total
VAR1	1.00	2	1	4	3
	2.00	2			2
9.00 (Missing)		3	2		5
Total		4	1	4	5

LOOKING AT THE PATTERN OF MISSING DATA ACROSS MANY VARIABLES

You can create a variable to display the pattern of missing data across many variables. Suppose you want to see the pattern of missing data across the numeric variables *v1, v2, v3,* and *v4.* The following code creates a new variable, *miss.ind,* which displays the pattern of missing values across these four variables:

```
* Create a variable to display missing data patterns.
DATA LIST /id v1 to v4 1-5.
BEGIN DATA
11323
24 32
32334
4 214
5 424
6 332
END DATA.
COMPUTE miss.1 = NOT(MISSING(v1)).
COMPUTE miss.2 = NOT(MISSING(v2)).
COMPUTE miss.3 = NOT(MISSING(v3)).
COMPUTE miss.4 = NOT(MISSING(v4)).
COMPUTE miss.ind = miss.1*1000 + miss.2*100 + miss.3*10
    + miss.4.
FORMATS miss.ind (N4.0).
FREQ VAR = miss.ind.
```

Output from the **FREQ** is presented in Table 17.5. The creation of the variable *miss.ind* takes advantage of the fact that **MISSING** is a logical function that takes the value of 1 if true and 0 if false. We have reversed the meaning of the **MISSING** function with the **NOT** keyword, so each logical variable (*miss.1* through *miss.4*) will have a value of 1 if the variable is not missing and 0 if it is missing. The four logical variables are then multiplied by constants so they will form a four-digit number. For instance, *miss.1* is multiplied by 1,000, so it will always appear as the first of four digits. Note that *miss.ind* must be formatted as **N4.0** rather than **F4.0** in order to have the leading zeros appear.

Table 17.5 Variable Displaying Missing-Data Patterns for Four Variables

		Frequency	Percent	Valid Percent	Cumulative Percent
Valid	0111	3	50.0	50.0	50.0
	1011	1	16.7	16.7	66.7
	1111	2	33.3	33.3	100.0
	Total	6	100.0	100.0	

CHANGING THE VALUE OF BLANKS IN NUMERIC FIELDS

By default, SPSS automatically assigns the system-missing value to blank fields in numeric variables. You can change this. For instance, you may want blanks coded as 0. This is demonstrated in the following syntax:

```
* Default setting: blanks = system-missing.
SET BLANKS = SYSMIS.
DATA LIST / v1 TO v4 1-4.
BEGIN DATA
1111
111
END DATA.
COMPUTE sum4 = v1 + v2 + v3 + v4.
LIST VARS = ALL.
* Set blanks equal to zero.
SET BLANKS = 0.
DATA LIST / v1 TO v4 1-4.
BEGIN DATA
1111
111
END DATA.
COMPUTE sum4 = v1 + v2 + v3 + v4.
LIST VARS = ALL.
```

This syntax reads the same data set twice, one with blanks set to the system-missing value and once with blanks set to 0. Output from the first **LIST** command, which displays results from the data set read with blanks set to system-missing, is presented in Table 17.6. There are two important points about these results:

1. The missing value of *v4* for the second case appears as a period (.), which signifies a system-missing value.

2. The variable *sum4* was not computed for the second case because one of the variables required for the calculation was missing.

Table 17.6   Blanks Read as System-Missing

V1	V2	V3	V4	SUM4
1	1	1	1	4.00
1	1	1	.	.

Table 17.7 displays results of the same calculations after the same data were read with blanks set to 0. This table differs in two ways from Table 17.6:

1. The missing value of *v4* for the second case appears as the value 0.
2. The variable *sum4* was computed for the second case because 0 is a valid value.

Table 17.7   Blanks Read as Zeros

V1	V2	V3	V4	SUM4
1	1	1	1	4.00
1	1	1	0	3.00

Several important points about the **SET BLANKS** command are as follows:

1. **SET BLANKS** applies to all numeric variables read or created after it is executed. It cannot be applied selectively.
2. The **SET** command cannot be applied retroactively, so it cannot change the system-missing value in the active file.
3. **SET** commands remain in force until changed. To restore the default setting and have blanks read as system-missing, use the command **SET BLANKS = SYSMIS**.
4. The **SET BLANKS** command does not affect string variables because they do not have system-missing values.

TREATMENT OF MISSING VALUES IN SPSS COMMANDS

Each SPSS command has a default setting for handling missing data, and many commands have one or more options besides the default. The default and available options are specified in the *SPSS 11.0 Syntax Reference Guide* (SPSS Inc., 2001), in the chapter on each command. The basic decisions to be made about missing data are

1. Will cases with missing data will be excluded from the analysis?
2. If cases are excluded, what method of exclusion will be used?

For the first question, the choice is whether to automatically exclude cases with missing values or to include them and treat missing values as a separate data value. For the second question, the choice is between listwise and casewise deletion. *Listwise* deletion excludes a case from analysis if it is missing on any variable used in the analysis. *Casewise* deletion, also known as *pairwise* deletion, excludes only cases that are missing on the specific variables required for each procedure. Consider the following example:

1. You want to produce a correlation matrix with three variables, *v1*, *v2*, and *v3*.

2. One case in the data set is missing on *v1* only, three cases are missing on *v2* only, and five cases are missing on *v3* only.

You have two options:

1. Use listwise deletion: Drop every case that is missing on any of the three variables. With this option, the same cases will be used to calculate each correlation, but your sample is reduced by nine cases.

2. Use casewise deletion: Use as many cases as possible for each paired correlation. This option uses the maximum possible data for each correlation but means that a different number of cases will be used to calculate each paired correlation, which can cause serious statistical problems. For more on this topic, see the Little and Rubin text mentioned earlier (2002).

SUBSTITUTING VALUES FOR MISSING DATA

Some people choose to deal with missing data by substituting a value calculated from the valid data on the same or related variables. This practice is controversial, and the programmer is, again, referred to Little and Rubin (2002). Several substitution techniques are presented here because programmers may want to use them. This is not an endorsement or a recommendation for their use.

One way to deal with missing data is to substitute the mean (average) value of a variable. Some procedures, such as **REGRESSION** and **FACTOR**, allow the programmer to request automatic mean substitution. This means that any cases missing on a variable will automatically be assigned the mean value as computed from the valid values for that variable. The substitute values are treated as observations so no cases are dropped from the analysis. If you have a file with 200 cases, 170 of which have complete data on *var1* to *var4*, the syntax,

```
REGRESSION VARIABLES = var1 var2 var3 var4
    / DEPENDENT = var1
    / METHOD = ENTER.
```

would use only the 170 complete cases, while

```
REGRESSION VARIABLES = var1 var2 var3 var4
    / DEPENDENT = var1
    / METHOD = ENTER
    / MISSING = MEANSUBSTITUTION.
```

would use all 200 cases. Of course, in the second instance, 30 cases would have data values that were not observed, but were computed from the values on other cases, so the validity of the results is open to question. Often, programmers will run the same analysis with and without mean substitution to see how much parameter estimates change. The substituted values created by this method are not written into the data file.

The **RMV** procedure may be used to substitute mean values for missing data, and it writes the new values into the data, which may then be used in any analysis. The command,

```
RMV newvar1 = smean(var1).
```

creates the variable *newvar1*, which will contain the value of *var1* if it exists for that case in the original data set, and the mean value of *var1* if *var1* is missing for that case. Table 17.8 shows how this would work for a hypothetical data set. The mean (3.17) of *var1* was written into *newvar1* for the two cases where *var1* was missing, and otherwise the values were copied from *var1* to *newvar1*.

It is also possible to write the substitute values into the original variables, as in the following syntax:

```
RMV var1 = smean(var1).
```

Table 17.8   Mean Substitution Using the **RMV** Command

CASE	VAR1	NEWVAR1
1	2.00	2.00
2	5.00	5.00
3	3.00	3.00
4	.	3.17
5	5.00	5.00
6	3.00	3.00
7	1.00	1.00
8	.	3.17

It is possible to control when mean substitution is applied, according to the number of cases missing on a variable. Suppose you have a scale of five items and wish to compute a summed-scale score for every case that has valid values on at least four of the items. Furthermore, you want to substitute a mean value for the one missing item for cases with four valid values. This may be expressed by the following rules:

1. If a case has valid values for all five items, compute the scale score from those values.
2. If a case has valid values for four of the five items, use mean substitution for the missing item and compute the scale score from the five values.
3. If a case has values for less than four items, make it missing on the scale score.

The steps to carry out this procedure are in the syntax below:

```
DATA LIST / v1 TO v5 1-5.
BEGIN DATA
11010
1110
101
END DATA.
* Count the number of missing values for v1-v5.
COMPUTE nmis5 = NMISS(v1 to v5).
* Calculate mean values for missing values.
RMV sv1 to sv5 = SMEAN(v1 to v5).
```

```
* Substitute mean values for cases missing exactly one
  item.
IF nmis5 = 1 AND MISSING(v1) v1 = sv1.
IF nmis5 = 1 AND MISSING(v2) v2 = sv2.
IF nmis5 = 1 AND MISSING(v3) v3 = sv3.
IF nmis5 = 1 AND MISSING(v4) v4 = sv4.
IF nmis5 = 1 AND MISSING(v5) v5 = sv5.
* Compute the scale using only complete cases,
  including substituted values.
COMPUTE scale = v1+v2+v3+v4+v5.
FORMAT nmis5 scale (F2.0).
LIST VAR = nmis5 scale.
```

This syntax reads a data set in which the first case has complete data, the second is missing on one variable, and the third is missing on two variables. It then performs the following tasks:

1. **COMPUTE nmis5 = NMISS(v1 to v5)**: This syntax creates the variable *nmis5*, which counts the number of missing variables for each case.

2. **RMV sv1 to sv5 = SMEAN(v1 to v5)**: This syntax creates five new variables, *sv1* to *sv5*, which hold mean values for the variables *v1* to *v5*.

3. **IF nmis5 = 1 AND MISSING(v1) v1 = sv1** to **IF nmis5 = 1 AND MISSING(v5) v5 = sv5**: These commands perform conditional mean substitution. For each variable *v1* to *v5*, if a case is missing on exactly one of these variables, the corresponding mean value is substituted for the mean value. For instance, if a case were missing on *v1* only, the value of *sv1* would be written into *v1*.

4. **COMPUTE scale = v1+v2+v3+v4+v5**: This syntax calculates the *scale* variable, whose value is the sum of the values *v1* to *v5*. This syntax takes advantage of the fact that any missing value in an arithmetic expression will cause the result to be missing (further discussed in Chapter 22). Therefore, it computes *scale* only for cases with complete data. Because this command follows the mean substitution procedure, cases with one missing variable are "complete" in the context of this command and the variable *scale* will be computed for them, while *scale* will not be computed for cases missing on more than one variable.

Output from the **LIST** command, presented in Table 17.9, demonstrates that *scale* was calculated for cases that were complete or missing one value, but not for cases missing more than one value. Note that if blanks are set equal to zero, there will be no missing values and this syntax will not work as intended. You can see the current setting for blanks in your system with the command **SHOW BLANKS,** and set blanks equal to system-missing (which will enable the syntax to work correctly) with the command **SET BLANKS = SYSMIS.**

Table 17.9   Results of Conditional Mean Substitution

NMISS	SCALE
0	3
1	3
2	.

CHAPTER 18

Using Random Processes in SPSS

This chapter discusses the use of random processes in SPSS, and the following topics:

○ The random-number seed

○ Generating random distributions

○ Selecting cases at random

SPSS has a pseudo-random number generator that allows you to generate random numbers from a specified distribution. Details about the algorithm used are available on the SPSS Web site (SPSS Technical Support). Pseudo-random numbers are not truly random, because they are generated by an algorithm and are dependent on a *seed*, or starting value, but are adequate for most purposes where the properties of randomness are desired.

THE RANDOM-NUMBER SEED

The seed value is set at the start of every SPSS session. Its initial value may vary or be fixed, depending on the installation. To see the seed in use, use the **SHOW SEED** command. By default, the seed value changes every time a random-number series is generated. To keep the same seed value for several series, run the **SET SEED** command before each series and specify the same seed number, for instance,

```
SET SEED = 123456789.
```

To have SPSS reset the seed to a random number, use the command,

```
SET SEED = RANDOM.
```

GENERATING RANDOM DISTRIBUTIONS

SPSS can generate data from many different distributions, including uniform, normal, and chi-square. A complete list may be found in the *SPSS 11.0 Syntax Reference Guide* (SPSS Inc., 2001), in the chapter on the **COMPUTE** command. Names of the functions used to generate random variables consist of the prefix **RV** for "random variable," a period (.), the name of or abbreviation for the distribution (e.g., **NORMAL** or **CHISQ**), and in parentheses, the information necessary to create the distribution, such as the range of a uniform distribution.

The **INPUT PROGRAM** command may be used to generate a data file from a specified distribution. The following syntax generates a data set consisting of 30 cases of one variable, *id*, whose values are generated from a normal distribution with a mean of 0 and standard deviation of 1:

```
SET SEED RANDOM.
INPUT PROGRAM.
LOOP id = 1 to 30.
COMPUTE id = RV.NORMAL(0,1).
END CASE.
END LOOP.
END FILE.
END INPUT PROGRAM.
EXE.
```

You do not need to have a data file open in the SPSS Data Editor window to run this program, because **INPUT PROGRAM** creates a new data set. This type of program can be used in classroom demonstrations, for instance, to show the effects of sample size on accuracy of estimation. By changing the second number in the **LOOP** command, you change the size of the sample drawn, so **LOOP id = 1 to 3000** will generate 3,000 values of *id*.

RANDOM SELECTION OF CASES

The SPSS command **SAMPLE** selects cases randomly from the active file. Sample size can be specified either as the number or the percentage of cases from the active file that should be selected. To draw a random sample of specified size, use code similar to the following:

```
SAMPLE 30 from 1000.
```

This will select exactly 30 cases for the sample if there are at least 1,000 cases in the active file. If there are more than 1,000 cases, the sample will be drawn from the first 1,000 cases only. If there are fewer than 1,000 cases, the sample will be proportionately smaller. For instance, if there are only 500 cases, approximately 15 will be selected. To select a proportion of cases rather than a specific number, use code similar to the following:

```
SAMPLE .25.
```

This will select approximately one quarter of the active file. Unless preceded by the **TEMPORARY** command, **SAMPLE** commands are permanent, so nonselected cases are deleted from the active file.

It is also possible to generate random numbers and use them for sampling. The following code creates a uniform random variable *random1* with a value between 0 and 1 for every case in the active file, then uses it to randomly select half the sample:

```
COMPUTE random1 = RV.UNIFORM(0,1).
SELECT IF random1 LE .5.
```

To select a fixed number of cases, use code similar to the following:

```
COMPUTE random1 = RV.UNIFORM(0,1).
RANK VARIABLES = random1
    / RANK into random2.
SELECT IF (random2 LE 30).
```

This code selects 30 cases at random from the active file by creating a uniform random variable, ranking cases on the value of that variable, then selecting the cases with the 30 lowest ranks.

RANDOM GROUP ASSIGNMENT

Cases may be randomly assigned to groups using a random variable. The following syntax randomly assigns cases within a data file so that approximately half will be in a treatment group and the other half in a control group:

```
COMPUTE random = RV.UNIF(0,1).
IF random LE .5 group = 1.
IF random GT .5 group = 2.
VAL LAB group 1 'treatment' 2 'control'.
EXE.
```

RANDOM SELECTION FROM MULTIPLE GROUPS

You can draw equal numbers of cases from several groups within a file, by ranking each group separately on the value of a random variable. The following code will draw samples of 25 men and 25 women (identified by the variable *gender*):

```
COMPUTE random = RV.UNIF(0,1).
RANK VARIABLES = random BY gender
    / RANK INTO rank2.
SELECT IF rank2 LE 25.
EXE.
```

A related circumstance is when cases are members of larger units and you want to select one case at random from each unit. Suppose you had a data set composed of individuals within households and each case had a value on the variable *house* that identified an individual's household. The following syntax ranks individuals randomly within each household and selects the individual with the lowest rank within his or her household:

```
COMPUTE random = uniform(1).
RANK VARIABLES = random by house.
SELECT IF rrandom = 1.
EXECUTE.
```

Note that the **SELECT** statement uses the default rank variable created by SPSS, *rrandom,* which consists of the letter *r* plus the name of the ranking variable, *random.*

Part V

Variables and Variable Manipulations

CHAPTER 19

Variables and Variable Formats

This chapter discusses different types of variables and variable formats used in SPSS, including

○ String and numeric variables

○ Scratch variables

○ Input and output formats

○ The **NUMBER** format

○ The **COMMA**, **DOT**, **DOLLAR**, and **PCT** formats

Logical variables, which take a value of true or false, are discussed in Chapter 21.

STRING AND NUMERIC VARIABLES

SPSS uses two types of variables: *string* and *numeric*. String variables are also called *alpha* or *alphanumeric* variables, because they can include both alphabetic characters (letters) and numbers. The following are some important points about string variables:

1. String variables are stored as a series of codes representing the individual characters in a character string, but they display as characters, for instance "Smith" or "10 Downing Street."

2. A string variable cannot be created through a function or procedure, but must be declared with the **STRING** command.

3. The length of a string variable cannot be changed through the **FORMATS**, **PRINT FORMATS**, or **WRITE FORMATS** commands.

4. String variables cannot be used in computation.

String variable functions are discussed in Chapter 23.

SPSS differentiates between *short string* and *long string* variables. Unless otherwise specified, references to string variables in this text refer to short string variables. Some important points about long and short string variables include the following:

1. The user does not declare string variables as long or short. This classification is done automatically and depends partly on the computer and operating system used.

2. The maximum length of a short string variable is typically 8 characters, while long string variables can hold up to 255 characters.

3. Short string variables can have user-missing values, but long string variables cannot.

4. Usually, long string variables are used to store lengthy blocks of text, such as free responses to questions, while short string variables are used to store values that fall into categories but were entered using text rather than numbers.

Numeric variables store numeric values and for this reason can be used in computations. Some important points about numeric variables include the following:

1. SPSS assumes variables are numeric unless they are declared otherwise.

2. Numeric variables are stored as floating-point numbers (as a base plus an exponent) but are usually displayed in other formats.

3. Numeric variables can contain only digits, periods, and the minus sign.

4. SPSS can read numeric variables in many different formats, such as integer binary and zoned decimal. These are described in the chapter on the **DATA LIST** command and in the "Variables" section of the "Universals" chapter in the *SPSS 11.0 Syntax Reference Guide* (SPSS Inc., 2001). Only the most common formats are discussed in this chapter.

Numeric variable functions are discussed in Chapter 22.

SYSTEM VARIABLES

Variables whose names begin with the dollar sign (**$**) are *system variables* and are created automatically by the SPSS system. Commonly used system variables include

○ **$CASENUM**, which is the sequence number of each case in a file.

○ **$SYSMIS**, which is the current value assigned to system-missing data.

○ **$TIME**, which is the number of seconds from October 14, 1582, to the present.

You cannot modify system variables, and they cannot be used in procedures, but they can be used in conditional and **COMPUTE** statements. Several chapters include syntax using system variables, including **$CASENUM** in Chapters 15 and 16 and **$TIME** in Chapter 24.

SCRATCH VARIABLES

Variables whose names begin with the pound sign (**#**) are *scratch variables.* This type of variable is created by the programmer and is not saved as part of the data file. Scratch variables are typically used when a variable is needed during a procedure, such as the counter variable in a **LOOP** command, but has no meaning outside that context. Use of scratch variables is demonstrated in Chapter 25 in conjunction with the **LOOP** command.

INPUT AND OUTPUT FORMATS

Every variable in SPSS has an input format and an output format. The *input format* affects how variables are read, while the *output format* controls how values are displayed or written to a file. Output formats are created at the same time as input formats and are usually identical to input formats at that time, although they can be changed later. The principal exceptions are some date formats (discussed in Chapter 24) and numeric variables displayed with nonnumeric symbols, such as commas (discussed later in this chapter). In both cases, the output format may be longer than the input format, to allow for the maximum length possible for a particular variable.

Output formats control how a variable appears but do not affect its stored value.

The output format of numeric variables can be changed through the **FORMATS**, **PRINT FORMATS**, and **WRITE FORMATS** commands. **FORMATS** is the most general of the three commands because it changes both print and write formats. The following syntax changes the output format of the variable *var1* to **F8.4**:

```
FORMATS var1 (F8.4).
```

The same basic structure is used for **PRINT FORMATS**, which affects how variables are displayed on the monitor or printed, and **WRITE FORMATS**, which controls how variables are written with the **WRITE** command. All three format commands take effect immediately.

Several variables may be formatted in the same **FORMATS** command, and they may be assigned different formats. It is optional to separate groups of variables by a slash (/), so the two commands below will function identically:

```
FORMATS var1 (F2.0) var2 var3 (F4.1).
FORMATS var1 (F2.0) / var2 var3 (F4.1).
```

The new format should include enough digits to display the largest value of the variable, including nonnumeric characters, such as commas. If it does not, SPSS will try to shorten the variable by dropping punctuation characters and decimal places. If the value is still too long to be displayed in the indicated format, a series of asterisks (***) will be displayed in its place. You can see the output formats of the variables in your file with the **DISPLAY VARIABLES** command. Most formats are easy to recognize because they follow these rules:

○ Most numeric variable formats have the form **Fw.d**, where **w** is the variable width and **d** is the number of digits to the right of the decimal point. The **F** stands for *floating point*, the format in which numeric variables are stored.

○ String variable formats have the form **Aw**, where **w** is the variable width. The **A** stands for *alphanumeric*, which is a synonym for *string* in this context.

○ Date and time variable formats have the form **NAMEw** or **NAMEw.d**, where **NAME** is the name of the specific format, **w** is the variable width, and **d** is the number of decimal places. Date and time variables are discussed further in Chapter 24.

○ A few numeric variable formats have the form **NAMEw** or **NAMEw.d**, where **NAME** is the name of the specific format, **w** is the variable width, and **d** is the number of decimal places. Examples include the **NUMBER**, **DOT**, **DOLLAR**, **PCT**, and **COMMA** formats discussed later in this chapter.

Table 19.1 may make these rules clearer. There are many other output formats available in SPSS. They are discussed in the *SPSS 11.0 Syntax Reference Guide* (SPSS Inc., 2001), in the **FORMATS** chapter and in the "Date and Time" section of the "Universals" chapter.

Table 19.1   Examples of SPSS Formats

Format	Meaning	Example
F2	Numeric, width 2, no decimal places	10
F4.2	Numeric, width 4, 2 decimal places	10.25
A3	String, width 3	abc
ADATE8	American date (mm/dd/yy), 2-digit year	01/20/03
PCT 6.2	Percent, width 6, 2 decimal places	25.25%

THE NUMBER FORMAT

Numeric variables stored with floating-point formats, such as **F8.2**, do not have leading zeros (zeros to the left of the meaningful digits, such as 0082). This is not a problem for numbers used in calculation, but it is a problem if you want to display a numeric variable with leading zeros. For instance, you may want to store an identification number as a numeric variable and also want this variable to be the same length for all cases. If this variable had values from 1 to 200, values less than 100 would need to be displayed with leading zeros, so 1 would be displayed as 001 and 20 as 020. The **NUMBER** format will allow you to do this because it automatically pads numeric variables with leading zeros up to the length of the variable. The following syntax illustrates use of the **NUMBER** format:

```
* Using the NUMBER format.
DATA LIST FREE / var1 var2.
BEGIN DATA
1 1
2 2
10 10
100 100
END DATA.
FORMAT var1 (N3.0).
LIST VARS = ALL.
```

Both *var1* and *var2* are read in the default numeric format, usually **F8.2**. The **FORMAT** command changes the format of *var1* to **NUMBER** format with a width of 3 and no decimal places (**N3.0**). This difference is clear in Table 19.2, which displays the output from the **LIST** command. The values of *var1* for the first three cases are padded with leading zeros so they have a width of 3, while the fourth case has three meaningful digits, so it is not padded. The values of *var2* appear in the default **F8.2** format.

Table 19.2   The **NUMBER** and **F8.2** Formats Contrasted

VAR1	VAR2
001	1.00
002	2.00
010	10.00
100	100.00

THE COMMA, DOT, DOLLAR, AND PCT FORMATS

The **COMMA**, **DOT**, **DOLLAR**, and **PCT** formats allow SPSS to perform two tasks:

1. Read numeric data containing certain nonnumeric symbols (commas, dollar signs, and percent signs)
2. Format variables using the specified symbols consistently, whether they were present in the original data or not

The **DOT** command performs a third task:

3. Interpret periods within data as the thousands separator, not the decimal point

Each of these formats may be used in two ways:

1. In a **DATA LIST** command, to control how raw data are read

2. In a **FORMATS** command, to control how variables are displayed

When used in the **DATA LIST** command, these formats should be used with the **FIXED** option and the variable width should be long enough to accommodate the extra characters (commas, dollar signs, etc.). These formats are demonstrated in the syntax below:

```
* Using the COMMA, DOT, DOLLAR, AND PERCENT FORMATS.
DATA LIST FIXED / var1 1-10 (COMMA) var2 11-20 (DOT)
  var3 21-30
(DOLLAR) var4 31-40 (PCT).
BEGIN DATA
100,000    100.000    $100,000    10%
200000     200000     200000      20
END DATA.
LIST VAR = ALL.
```

Output from the **LIST** command is presented in Table 19.3. Note that these input formats also standardize the output formats: The variables for the second case appear with commas, decimal points, dollar signs, and percent signs, although those symbols were not present in the raw data. The values of *var2* are 100,000 and 200,000 because in the **DOT** format, the period is the thousands separator, not the decimal point.

Table 19.3   Data Read Using the **COMMA, DOT, DOLLAR,** and **PERCENT** Formats

VAR1	VAR2	VAR3	VAR4
100,000	100.000	$100,000	10%
200,000	200.000	$200.000	20%

The following syntax demonstrates using the **COMMA, DOT, DOLLAR,** and **PCT** formats to change the output format of numeric variables in an SPSS system file:

```
DATA LIST FREE / v1 v2 v3 v4.
BEGIN DATA
1000 2000 300 40.0
END DATA.
LIST VAR = ALL.
FORMAT v1 (COMMA8) v2 (DOT8) v3 (DOLLAR8) v4 (PCT6.1).
LIST VAR = ALL.
```

Table 19.4 displays the output from the first **LIST** command, which shows the variables in the default **F8.2** format. Table 19.5 displays the output from the second **LIST** command, after the specific formats have been applied.

Table 19.4   Data Displayed in the **F8.2** Formats

V1	V2	V3	V4
1000.00	2000.00	300.00	40.00

Table 19.5   Data Displayed in the **COMMA, DOT, DOLLAR,** and **PERCENT** Formats

V1	V2	V3	V4
1,000	2.000	$300	40.0%

CHAPTER 20

Variable and Value Labels

This chapter discusses variable names and labels and value labels. Specific topics include

○ Rules about variable names in SPSS

○ Systems for naming variables

○ Adding variable labels

○ Adding value labels

○ Controlling whether labels are displayed in tables

○ Applying the data dictionary from a previous data set

RULES ABOUT VARIABLE NAMES IN SPSS

Before SPSS 12.0, names of SPSS variables were limited to 8 characters. Even though Version 12.0 allows variable names of up to 64 characters, many programmers will continue to adhere to the 8-character limit, at least for the near future, so their programs will be compatible with earlier versions of SPSS. Besides the length limit, the following rules apply to SPSS variable names:

1. They must begin with a letter or one of the symbols @, #, or $.

2. Only letters, numbers, the period (.), underscore (_), and the $, #, and @ symbols can be used within variable names.

3. Spaces are not allowed within variable names.

When files imported from other programs have variable names that violate these rules, SPSS alters the names according to the following:

1. Variable names longer than eight characters will be truncated to eight characters.

2. Names containing spaces have an underscore added where the spaces were.

3. Names violating other SPSS naming conventions or that would duplicate other names after truncation are renamed *v1, v2,* and so on according to their positions in the original file.

SYSTEMS FOR NAMING VARIABLES

Every variable in an SPSS data set has a name, even if it is the default name assigned by the system, such as *var00001, var00002,* and so on in the current Macintosh and PC versions of SPSS. Most programmers choose to assign names to the variables in their data sets. There are two schools of thought on variable names: Some people believe the name itself should be informative, while others prefer to use simple consecutive variable names (such as *v1, v2, v3*). The principal advantage to using meaningful names is that they suggest what the variable means. Consider how easy it is to grasp the meaning of the first line of code below, while the second requires reference to a codebook to find the meaning of the variables:

```
COMPUTE income = wages + bonus + tips.
COMPUTE v4 = v1 + v2 + v3.
```

Using consecutive variable names has two principal advantages: They are easier to type, and it is easier to find variables in a questionnaire or other document if they are consecutively numbered.

SPSS variable names are not case-sensitive: SPSS will treat *VAR1* and *var1* as the same variable name. Both the Macintosh and PC versions of SPSS translate variable names to capital letters in output tables, so this book follows that convention in presenting output, although variable names are presented in lowercase letters in syntax and in narrative text.

ADDING VARIABLE LABELS

Variable labels allow you to attach descriptive text to variables and can be displayed in the output from some procedures as well as or instead of variable names. The syntax below attaches the label 'Pupil' to *v1* and 'School' to *v2:*

```
VARIABLE LABELS v1 'Pupil' / v2 'School'.
```

If multiple variables are labeled with a single command, they must be separated by slashes, as in the example above. The apostrophes around the variable labels are optional unless the label continues over more than one line. Variable labels may be as long as 255 characters, although they will be truncated in the output from some procedures. Variable labels become part of the dictionary attached to the data file, and when the command **VARIABLE LABELS** is applied to a variable that had a label previously, the old label will be replaced by the new. Any character, including blanks, can be included within a variable label. If a label includes an apostrophe, the label must be enclosed with quotation marks.

Variable labels can be continued across command lines, but each segment of the label must be enclosed in apostrophes or quotation marks, and a plus sign (**+**) must appear at the beginning of each continuation line, followed immediately by the continuation of the label. These rules are illustrated in the following example:

```
VARIABLE LABELS exam1 "First exam taken in subject's"
+" freshman year".
```

ADDING VALUE LABELS

Sometimes, the meaning of values in a variable is clear. For instance, the value '45' in a variable labeled *age* probably refers to a 45-year-old person. However, often values are codes that need further explanation. For instance, '1' may signify 'Yes' and '0' may signify 'No.' Using numeric codes rather than text fields has several advantages, including easier data entry. The major disadvantage of using numeric codes is that their meaning is not self-evident. The **VALUE LABELS** command allows you to attach meaningful labels to numeric codes, and this information is added to the dictionary for the data file. The following syntax adds the label 'Yes' to the value 1 and 'No' to the value 0 for the variable *v1* to *v5*.

```
VALUE LABELS v1 to v5 1 'Yes' 0 'No'.
```

Value labels may be applied to numeric or short string variables but not to long string variables (long and short string variables are discussed in Chapter 19). Value labels can hold up to 60 characters, although only 20 characters will be displayed by most SPSS procedures. As with variable labels, if a value label is continued over several lines, each segment must be enclosed in quotation marks or apostrophes and a plus (+) used before each segment except the first. Value labels must be enclosed in apostrophes or quotation marks, and if labels are being added to a short string variable, the values themselves must also be enclosed in quotation marks or apostrophes.

A **VALUE LABELS** command deletes existing value labels for the variables named. To add additional value labels without deleting those that already exist, use the **ADD VALUE LABELS** command. The syntax below uses the **VALUE LABELS** and **ADD VALUE LABELS** commands for the same variable:

```
VALUE LABELS v1 0 'No'.
ADD VALUE LABELS v1 1 'Yes'.
```

This syntax will result in variable *v1* having the label 'No' for value 0 and 'Yes' for value 1.

CONTROLLING WHETHER LABELS ARE DISPLAYED IN TABLES

If you have attached labels to variables and values in a data file, you can have them appear in tabular output instead of or as well as the variable names and values. This is accomplished through the **SET** command. For instance,

```
SET TVARS = LABELS.
```

will have the variable labels rather than the names appear, and,

```
SET TNUMBERS = BOTH.
```

will have both values and value labels appear. **TNUMBERS** and **TVALUES** stand for *table numbers* and *table values,* respectively. Despite the name, the **TNUMBERS** option applies to string values as well. The options for variables are **NAMES**, **LABELS**, or **BOTH**; for values, they are **VALUES**, **LABELS**, or **BOTH**. You can find the current settings with the command,

```
SHOW TVARS TNUMBERS.
```

APPLYING THE DATA DICTIONARY FROM A PREVIOUS DATA SET

The **APPLY DICTIONARY** command allows you to copy dictionary information (variable labels, value labels, missing values, print and write formats, and weights) from an SPSS system file (the *source file*) to a new file (the *target file*). The target file must be the active file when the **APPLY DICTIONARY** command is executed. The following syntax will apply the dictionary information from the system file *source.sav* to the active file:

```
APPLY DICTIONARY FROM 'source.sav'.
```

The following rules govern how dictionary information is applied to the target file:

1. Dictionary information will be applied to every variable in the target file that has the same name and type as a variable in the source file. Variables in the target file that have no matches in the source file are not changed.

2. If a variable has a label in the target file but not in the source file or if the source file label is a blank, the label from the target file will be retained.

3. Value labels for each variable are treated as a set: If a variable in the source file has any value labels, the set of labels from the source file will replace the set of value labels in the target file.

4. Missing-value designations for each variable are treated as a set: If a variable in the source file has any missing-value designations, they will replace the set of missing values designated in the target file for that variable.

5. Print and write formats of matched numeric variables in the target file are changed to those of the source file, while string variables are left unchanged.

6. Weight information from the target file is retained if the source file is unweighted, and copied from the source file if it is weighted, and the weight variable from the source file is matched in the target file.

⊞ CHAPTER 21

Recoding and Creating Variables

This chapter discusses different ways to recode variables in SPSS and ways to create new variables. Specific topics discussed include the following:

○ The **IF** statement

○ Relational operators

○ Logical variables

○ Logical operators

○ Creating dummy variables

○ The **RECODE** and **AUTORECODE** commands

○ Converting variables from string to numeric or numeric to string

○ Counting the occurrence of values across variables

○ Counting the occurrence of multiple values in one variable

○ Creating a cumulative variable

Frequently, you will want to change the values of certain variables in a data set, for instance, to categorize continuous values or reverse the scoring on questionnaire items. You may also wish to create new variables using the information contained in other variables. For instance, you may want to create a set of indicator or dummy variables that reflect the information contained in a single variable with many categories. SPSS offers several different methods of recoding values, most notably the **IF** and **RECODE** commands. Other ways to recode variables are presented in Chapter 25, which discusses the **DO IF**, **DO REPEAT**, and **LOOP** commands.

THE IF STATEMENT

An **IF** statement or command specifies an action to be taken, conditional on the value of some logical expression. An **IF** statement has three components: a relational or logical expression, a target variable, and an assignment expression. In the following syntax,

```
IF (var1= 1 AND var2 > 50) group = 2.
```

the logical expression is **var1 = 1 AND var2 > 50**, the target variable is **group**, and the assignment expression is **= 2**. The logical expression may be either true or false. If it is true, the target variable will be recoded according to the assignment expression. If it is false, the assignment expression will not be executed and the target variable either retains its current value (if the target variable existed before the **IF** command was executed) or is missing (if the target variable did not).

The terms *logical expression* or *relational expression* are often used synonymously. In this context, they refer to an expression that states a relationship between two entities and may be either true or false. In this example, we used a compound expression, which consists of two *relational statements* (**var1 = 1** and **var2 > 50**) joined by a *logical operator* (**AND**). The parentheses are optional in this case but were included to make the syntax easier to read. Relational statements and logical operators are discussed further later in this chapter. However, their meaning is often intuitive: In this case, the logical statement **var1 = 1 AND var2 > 50** is true if both conditions are met (i.e., if the value of *var1* is equal to 1 and the value of *var2* is greater than 50).

RELATIONAL OPERATORS

A *relational operator* states a relationship between variables or constants, for instance, that they are equal or that the first is greater than the second. Table 21.1 displays the relational operators that are used with the **IF** command. The symbols and abbreviations are interchangeable, so the two statements below will function identically:

```
IF var1 GT 25 var2 EQ 1.
IF var1 > 25 var2 = 1.
```

Table 21.1   SPSS Relational Operators

Meaning	Symbol	Abbreviation
Equal to	=	EQ
Less than	<	LT
Greater than	>	GT
Not equal to*	<>	NE
Less than or equal to	<=	LE
Greater than or equal to	>=	GE

* On some systems you can use the symbols ~= for "Not equal to."

The following rules apply to relational expressions in SPSS:

○ String variables can be compared only to string variables or string constants, and numeric variables to numeric variables or numeric constants.

○ String variables cannot be created in a logical expression.

○ String values must be enclosed in apostrophes or quotation marks.

○ Each relational expression must be completely stated, so the first line of the following syntax is incorrect, while the second is correct:

```
IF state = "ND" OR "SD" region = "North
   Central".                                    [WRONG]
IF state = "ND" OR state = "SD" region = "North
   Central".
```

The following syntax demonstrates the use of relational operators in **IF** statements:

```
* Relational operators.
DATA LIST FREE / var1.
BEGIN DATA
25 26 27 28 29 30
END DATA.
IF var1 < 25 r1 = 1.
IF var1 <= 25 r2 = 1.
IF var1 NE 28 r3 = 1.
IF var1 GE 29 r4 = 1.
FORMATS var1 to r4 (F2.0).
LIST VAR = ALL.
```

In this syntax, if a logical expression is true, the outcome variable (*r1*, *r2*, *r3*, or *r4*) is assigned a value of 1. If the logical expression is false, the outcome variable is missing. The first logical expression (**var1 < 25**) is false for all values in the data set, so the assignment expression **r1 = 1** is never executed and all cases are missing on *r1*. The logical expression of the second **IF** statement (**var1 <= 25**) is true for the first case, so that case has a value of 1 for *r2*, while the other cases are missing on *r2*. Coding for *r3* and *r4* follows the same pattern, as can be seen in Table 21.2, which displays the output from the **LIST** command.

Table 21.2   Variables Created With **IF** Statements

VAR1	R1	R2	R3	R4
25	.	1	1	.
26	.	.	1	.
27	.	.	1	.
28	.	.	.	.
29	.	.	1	1
30	.	.	1	1

LOGICAL VARIABLES

Logical variables take the value 1 if true, 0 if false, and missing if they can't be evaluated. The syntax below creates a set of logical variables *log1* to *log4*, analogous to the variables *r1* to *r4* in the previous syntax:

```
DATA LIST FREE / var1.
BEGIN DATA
25 26 27 28 29 30
END DATA.
COMPUTE log1 = var1 < 25.
COMPUTE log2 = var1 <= 25.
COMPUTE log3 = var1 NE 28.
COMPUTE log4 = var1 GE 29.
FORMAT ALL (F2.0).
LIST VAR = ALL.
```

Table 21.3, which presents the results of the **LIST** command, is identical to Table 21.2, except that missing values in Table 21.2 have the value 0 in Table 21.3. This is because a logical variable with the value of false (i.e., that was created by a false logical expression), takes the value of 0.

Table 21.3   Logical Variables Created With the **COMPUTE** Command

VAR1	LOG1	LOG2	LOG3	LOG4
25	0	1	1	0
26	0	0	1	0
27	0	0	1	0
28	0	0	0	0
29	0	0	1	1
30	0	0	1	1

The fact that 1 = true and 0 = false for logical variables can be used to create new variables. Suppose you work for a health insurance company and have a data file that identifies claims by two variables: *days*, which is the number of days claimed, and *type*, which identifies the type of claim. For instance, a particular claim might be for 5 days of inpatient hospital services or 1 day of outpatient services. The syntax below creates new variables that contain the number of days claimed for each type of service:

```
* Creating new variables using logical variables.
DATA LIST FREE / days (F2.0) type (A).
BEGIN DATA
1 I
```

```
3 I
6 O
10 I
5 O
END DATA.
COMPUTE indays = days*(type = 'I').
COMPUTE outdays = days*(type = 'O').
FORMAT indays outdays (F2.0).
LIST VARS = ALL.
```

This syntax creates two new variables: *indays*, which holds the number of inpatient days for a particular claim, and *outdays*, which holds the number of outpatient days for a claim. The logical value of the **type = 'I'** and **type = 'O'** statements control the creation of the *indays* and *outdays* variables. For instance, for the first case, the logical statement **type = 'I'** was true, so the value of *days* was multiplied by 1 and the result written into *indays*. The logical statement **type = 'O'** was false for the first case, so the value of days was multiplied by 0 and the result written into *outdays*. Output from the **LIST** command is displayed in Table 21.4.

Table 21.4   Variables Created Using Logical Variables as Multipliers

DAYS	TYPE	INDAYS	OUTDAYS
1	I	1	0
3	I	3	0
6	O	0	6
10	I	10	0
5	O	0	5

LOGICAL OPERATORS

Logical operators, also known as *Boolean operators,* are used to combine relational or logical statements into complex logical expressions. When several relational statements are linked in a logical expression, the truth or falsity of the entire expression is evaluated. Table 21.5 presents the logical operators that can be used with the **IF** command.

Table 21.5   SPSS Logical Operators

OPERATOR	SYMBOL*	MEANING
AND	&	and
OR	|	or
NOT	~	not

* ~ is not available on all systems.

The basic rules governing the evaluation of complex logical statements are simple:

○ For an **AND** statement to be true, all parts must be true.

○ For an **OR** statement to be true, it suffices for one part to be true.

SPSS evaluates relational statements joined by Boolean operators, as displayed in Table 21.6. Table 21.7 displays how SPSS evaluates logical expressions including missing data.

Table 21.6   SPSS Evaluation of Logical Expressions

A	B	relational statements	values	outcome
30	25	(A=30) AND (B=25)	true AND true	true
30	25	(A=30) AND (B=30)	true AND false	false
30	25	(A=20) AND (B=30)	false AND false	false
30	25	(A=30) OR (B=30)	true OR false	true
30	25	(A=20) OR (B=20)	false OR false	false

Table 21.7   SPSS Evaluation of Logical Expressions Including Missing Data

A	B	C	D	logical statements	values	outcome
30	25	.	.	(A=30) AND (C=25)	true AND missing	missing
30	25	.	.	(C=30) AND (D=25)	missing AND missing	missing
30	25	.	.	(C=30) AND (B=30)	missing AND false	false
30	25	.	.	(A=30) OR (C=25)	true OR missing	true
30	25	.	.	(A= 20) OR (C=25)	false OR missing	missing
30	25	.	.	(C= 20) OR (D=25)	missing OR missing	missing

As mentioned earlier, parentheses are not always required in logical statements, but they can clarify the meaning of the syntax. When two or more logical operators are used within a single statement, parentheses can be used to change the order of operations. SPSS evaluates the logical statements within a command in the following order:

1. **NOT**

2. **AND**

3. **OR**

It is possible to rely on the order of operations in complex logical statements, but using parentheses can clarify syntax. For instance, the following two statements are equivalent:

a = 1 AND b = 2 OR c = 3 AND D = 4.
(a = 1 AND b = 2) OR (c = 3 AND D = 4).

but adding the parentheses makes it clear what the programmer intended and removes any suspicion that the following statement may have been intended instead:

a = 1 AND (b = 2 OR c = 3) AND D = 4.

CREATING DUMMY VARIABLES

Often, a data set contains variables that need to be recoded as a series of *indicator* or *dummy variables.* These are variables that indicate the absence or presence of some characteristic. For instance, you may have a variable named *race,* with three categories: 1 = White, 2 = Black, 3 = Other. The values of this variable have meaning only at the nominal level, as labels indicating what racial group a person identifies with. To use the information contained in this variable in a regression equation, you need to recode it into dummy variables. There are different schemes to accomplish this type of recoding. A simple method is illustrated here, in which 1 indicates the presence of a characteristic and 0 its absence. We will create three new variables, *White, Black,* and *Other,* each with a value of 1 if that category applies to the case, and 0 otherwise. The following syntax accomplishes this using logical variables:

```
DATA LIST FREE / race.
BEGIN DATA
1 1 2 3 3 2 2 1
END DATA.
COMPUTE White = (race = 1).
COMPUTE Black = (race = 2).
COMPUTE Other = (race = 3).
FORMAT race to Other (F2.0).
LIST VAR = ALL.
```

Results of the **LIST** command are presented in Table 21.8. The **DO REPEAT** command can also be used to create dummy variables, as discussed in Chapter 25.

Table 21.8   Dummy Variables Created Using Logical Statements

RACE	WHITE	BLACK	OTHER
1	1	0	0
1	1	0	0
2	0	1	0
3	0	0	1
3	0	0	1
2	0	1	0
2	0	1	0
1	1	0	0

THE RECODE AND AUTORECODE COMMANDS

The **RECODE** command allows you to recode values within a variable or on multiple variables, also known as the *input* variables, and can write the recoded values to new variables, also known as *target* variables. In the **RECODE** statement that follows, **var1** and **var3** are the input variables; the assignment statements **(2=0) (ELSE = COPY)** specify how they should be recoded; and **var1r** and **var2r** are the target variables:

```
RECODE var1 var2 (2=0) (ELSE = COPY) INTO var1r var2r.
```

Once this code is executed, any case with a value of 2 on *var1* will have a value of 0 on *var1r*, while otherwise *var1* and *var1r* will have the same values. The same rules apply to *var2r*. Values for string variables must be enclosed in quotes or apostrophes, for example,

```
RECODE string1 string2 ('A' = '1') ('B' = '2').
```

This syntax does not name target variables, so the values of *string1* and *string2* will be overwritten (i.e., replaced by the new values).

The keywords **LO** or **LOWEST**, **HI** or **HIGHEST**, and **THRU** can be used to specify value ranges for numeric variables. In the example below, the acceptable range of values for *var1* and *var2* is 1 through 3, so values outside that range are recoded as system-missing:

```
DATA LIST FREE / var1 var2.
BEGIN DATA
0 1 1 3 1 4 2 2
END DATA.
LIST VAR = ALL.
RECODE var1 var2 (LO THRU .99 = sysmis) (3.01 THRU HI
= SYSMIS)
(ELSE = COPY) into var1x var2x.
FORMATS ALL (F2.0).
LIST VAR = var1 var1x var2 var2x.
```

Results from the **LIST** command are presented in Table 21.9. After recoding, the target variables are missing for the out-of-range values in the first and third cases, and otherwise have the same values as the input variables.

Table 21.9   Data With Out-of-Range Values Recoded to MISSING

VAR1	VAR1X	VAR2	VAR2X
0	.	1	1
1	1	3	3
1	1	4	.
2	2	2	2

The **AUTORECODE** command automatically assigns consecutive integers to the values of input variables and writes the new values to target variables. Input variables for **AUTORECODE** can be either string or numeric, but target variables are always numeric. The value labels or values from the original variables become value labels in the target variables. A common use of **AUTORECODE** is to create consecutive integer values for variables to be used in procedures such as **ONEWAY** or **ANOVA**. The following syntax demonstrates the use of **AUTORECODE**:

```
* Demonstrating the AUTORECODE command.
DATA LIST FREE / schoolid (F2.0) status (A15).
BEGIN DATA
5 Dropout
5 Graduated
17 Dropout
17 Transferred
32 Graduated
32 Graduated
32 Transferred
END DATA.
AUTORECODE schoolid status / INTO rschool rstatus.
LIST VAR = schoolid rschool status rstatus.
```

Results of the **LIST** command are presented in Table 21.10. The input variables are *schoolid* and *status,* and the target variables are *rschool* and *rstatus.* Autorecode values are assigned by the sort order of the input values. For instance, for the string variable *status,* the value 'Dropout' was autorecoded to 1 because it comes first in alphabetical order. For the numeric variable *schoolid,* the value 5 was autorecoded to 1 because it comes first in numerical order.

Table 21.10 Variables Created With the **AUTORECODE** Command

SCHOOLID	RSCHOOL	STATUS	RSTATUS
5	1	Dropout	1
5	1	Graduated	2
17	2	Dropout	1
17	2	Transferred	3
32	3	Graduated	2
32	3	Graduated	2
32	3	Transferred	3

CONVERTING VARIABLES FROM
NUMERIC TO STRING OR STRING TO NUMERIC

It is easy to convert a variable from numeric to string variable, because all numeric values are valid string values. The following code demonstrates this process:

```
* Converting numeric variables to string.
DATA LIST FREE / var1 (F2.0).
BEGIN DATA
1 2 14 5 17
END DATA.
STRING svar1 (A2).
COMPUTE svar1 = STRING(var1,F2.0).
LIST VAR = ALL.
```

This code creates a data set with one numeric variable, *var1*, then uses the string function to convert it to the string variable *svar1*. The format in the **STRING** function **(F2.0)** is that of the source variable, not the target variable. Output from the **LIST** command is presented in Table 21.11.

Table 21.11 Numeric Variable Converted to String

VAR1	SVAR1
1	1
2	2
14	14
5	5
17	17

Converting string variables to numeric is more complicated because not all valid string values are valid numeric values. The simplest case is converting string variables that include only digits (i.e., representations of numbers, rather than alphabetic or other characters). Two ways to perform this conversion are demonstrated in the following syntax:

```
* Converting string variables to numeric (1).
* The easy case, when the string variables contain only
  digits.
DATA LIST FREE / svar (A2).
BEGIN DATA
1 2 14 5 17
END DATA.
* First method.
RECODE svar (CONVERT) INTO num1.
* Second method.
COMPUTE num2 = NUMBER(svar,F2.0).
FORMATS num1 num2 (F2.0).
LIST VAR = ALL.
```

This syntax creates a data set with one string variable, *svar*, then uses two different techniques to convert it into the numeric variables *num1* and *num2*. The first method uses a **RECODE** statement with the **CONVERT** keyword, which specifies that the string values in *svar* should be converted to numeric values before being written to the variable *num1*. It is not necessary to name specific values or use the keywords **ELSE = COPY** in this case. The second method uses a **COMPUTE** command with the **NUMBER** function. Although the argument to the **NUMBER** function is the source string variable *(svar)*, the format specified **(F2.0)** is that of the target numeric variable. Output from the **LIST** is presented in Table 21.12.

Table 21.12   String Variable Converted to Numeric (1)

SVAR	NUM1	NUM2
1	1	1
2	2	2
14	14	14
5	5	5
17	17	17

The two methods demonstrated above for converting string variables to numeric work only for string values that are representations of numbers. To have numeric values assigned to string values such as 'A' or '+,' you must use the **RECODE** command and specify how to translate values between the target and source variables. This is demonstrated in the following syntax:

```
* Converting string variables to numeric (2).
* The more difficult case, when the strings include
  letters and symbols.
DATA LIST FREE / svar2 (A2).
BEGIN DATA
1 3 A 2 #
END DATA.
RECODE svar2 ('A'= 10) ('#'= 11) (CONVERT) INTO num3.
LIST VAR = ALL.
```

The **CONVERT** keyword on the **RECODE** command will translate representations of numbers in the variable *svar2* to numbers in the variable *num3*. Conversion of the other symbols is specified by the **('A'= 10)** and **('#'= 11)** assignment statements. Output from the **LIST** command is presented in Table 21.13.

Table 21.13   String Variable Converted to Numeric (2)

SVAR2	NUM3
1	1.00
3	3.00
A	10.00
2	2.00
#	11.00

COUNTING OCCURRENCES
OF VALUES ACROSS VARIABLES

The **COUNT** command allows you to create a variable that counts the number of occurrences of a value or values across two or more variables. For instance, you may have a set of 10 variables representing data from a questionnaire, each with the possible values 1 "Strongly agree," 2 "Agree," 3 "No opinion," 4 "Disagree," and 5 "Strongly disagree." The following code will create the count variable *strdis*, which counts how many times each subject chose the response "Strongly disagree" (value 5) on *var1* to *var10:*

```
* Creating a COUNT variable.
DATA LIST FREE / id v1 to v10.
```

```
BEGIN DATA
1 1 1 2 3 2 1 3 4 3 4
2 2 2 3 4 1 5 5 4 5 4
3 2 3 3 5 2 4 4 5 5 5
END DATA.
COUNT strdis = v1 TO v10 (5).
FORMATS id TO strdis (F2.0).
LIST VAR = id strdis.
```

Results from the **LIST** command are displayed in Table 21.14. The first subject never chose "Strongly disagree," the second chose it three times, and the third chose it four times.

Table 21.14   Data Set With Count Variable

ID	STRDIS
1	0
2	3
3	4

COUNTING THE OCCURRENCE OF MULTIPLE VALUES IN ONE VARIABLE

The **ANY** function searches for the appearance of specified values within one variable and takes the logical value of *true* or 1 if any of them are found, and *false* or 0 otherwise. The following two commands are equivalent:

```
IF ANY(var1,2,4,6,8) flag = 1.
IF var1 = 2 OR var1 = 4 OR var1 = 6 OR var1 = 8
flag = 1.
```

The first argument to the **ANY** function is the name of the variable to be searched (**var1** in the above example), and the remaining arguments are the values to be searched for, separated by commas (**2,4,6,8** in the above example). When the **ANY** function is used with a string variable, values to be searched for must be enclosed in quotation marks or apostrophes, the target variable must be string, and the target value must be enclosed in quotation marks or apostrophes, as in the following example:

```
IF ANY(string1,"a""c") string2 = "1".
```

CREATING A CUMULATIVE VARIABLE

There are several ways to create a cumulative variable containing the sum of the values of some other variable across many cases. One method is to use the **LEAVE** command, which keeps the value of the cumulative variable from being reinitialized as each new case is read. This technique is demonstrated in the following syntax, which creates a cumulative variable, *cumsales*, containing the sum of *sales* for all cases in the data set:

```
* Creating a cumulative variable with the LEAVE
  command.
DATA LIST FREE / id sales.
BEGIN DATA
1 5 2 10 3 5 4 20 5 10
END DATA.
COMPUTE cumsales = cumsales + sales.
LEAVE cumsales.
EXE.
FORMAT ALL (F2.0).
LIST VAR = ALL.
```

This syntax writes the value of *sales* for the first case to *cumsales*, then adds the value of *sales* to *cumsales* as each new case is read. When the first case is read, the value of *cumsales* is 5, the same as the value of *sales* for the first case. When the second case is read, the value of *cumsales* becomes 15, which is the sum of the values of *sales* for the first and second cases. When the final case in the file is read, the value of *cumsales* is 50, equal to the sum of *sales* for all the cases in the file. Output from the **LIST** command is presented in Table 21.15.

Table 21.15 Data Set With Cumulative Variable

ID	SALES	CUMSALES
1	5	5
2	10	15
3	5	20
4	20	40
5	10	50

Another way to create a cumulative variable is with the **LAG** function, as demonstrated in the following syntax:

```
* Creating a cumulative variable with the LAG function.
DATA LIST FREE / id sales.
BEGIN DATA
1 5 2 10 3 5 4 20 5 10
END DATA.
DO IF $CASENUM = 1.
COMPUTE cumsales = sales.
ELSE.
COMPUTE cumsales = LAG(cumsales) + sales.
END IF.
EXE.
FORMAT ALL (F2.0).
LIST VAR = ALL.
```

The output produced by the **LIST** command will be identical to that presented in Table 21.15. This syntax uses the **LAG** function to add the value of *sales* for each case to the value of *cumsales*, so that when all cases are read, *cumsales* equals the total value of *sales* for all cases. The **LAG** function is discussed further in Chapter 16.

CHAPTER 22

Numeric Operations and Functions

This chapter discusses numeric operations and functions in SPSS, including

○ Arithmetic operations

○ Mathematical and statistical functions

○ Missing values in arithmetic operations and functions

○ Domain errors

○ A substring-like technique for numeric variables

This chapter introduces the concept of a function in SPSS and discusses operations and functions for numeric variables. Functions for string variables are discussed in Chapter 23.

ARITHMETIC OPERATIONS

The basic mathematical operations of addition, subtraction, multiplication, division, and exponentiation can be written into SPSS syntax using symbols called *operators*. The operators available in SPSS are presented in Table 22.1.

Table 22.1   SPSS Mathematical Operators

Operator	Meaning
+	Addition
−	Subtraction
*	Multiplication
/	Division
**	Exponentiation

Use of these operators in **COMPUTE** statements is fairly intuitive, as is demonstrated in the following syntax:

```
DATA LIST FREE / v1 v2 v3 v4.
BEGIN DATA
1 2 3 4
5 6 7 8
END DATA.
COMPUTE add = v1 + v2.
compute add2 = v1 + v2 + v3.
COMPUTE subtr = v2 - v1.
COMPUTE mult = v3 * v4.
COMPUTE divide = v4 / v2.
COMPUTE expon = v2 ** 2.
FORMAT v1 to mult expon (F2.0).
LIST VAR = add to expon.
```

Results from the **LIST** command are presented in Table 22.2.

Table 22.2   Variables Created Using Mathematical Operators

ADD	ADD2	SUBTR	MULT	DIVIDE	EXPON
3	6	1	12	2.00	4
11	18	1	56	1.33	36

If more than one type of arithmetic operation is included on a **COMPUTE** statement, the operations will be executed according to the following order of operations:

1. Functions

2. Exponentiation

3. Multiplication

4. Division

5. Addition and subtraction

Operations on the same level, for instance, two multiplication statements, are executed from left to right. Operations in parentheses are executed first and override the default order of operations. Even if your syntax uses the default order of operations, it is often useful to include parentheses to clarify the order of operations. If several expressions on a **COMPUTE** statement are nested within parentheses, they are executed beginning with the innermost expression and working outward.

MATHEMATICAL AND STATISTICAL FUNCTIONS

A complete list of SPSS mathematical and statistical functions is available in the **COMPUTE** chapter of the *SPSS 11.0 Syntax Reference Guide* (SPSS Inc., 2001). Only the most common functions will be demonstrated here. All functions have the same parts:

1. The *name* of the function

2. The *arguments* to the function, contained within parentheses

The basic meaning of a function is "Do this operation (name of function) on these variables or values (arguments of the function)." For instance, the function **SQRT(var2)** tells SPSS to compute the square root of *var2:* The name of the function is **SQRT**, and the argument is *var2.*

Functions may have multiple arguments, and arguments may be variables, constants, or both. For instance, the function **SUM(5,10,15)** has three arguments, all of which are constants (the numbers 5, 10, and 15). The function **SUM(5,v2)** has two arguments: One is a constant (the number 5), and one is a variable *(v2).*

Functions may be nested; that is, the result of one function may be used as an argument to another function. The following rules apply to nested functions:

1. Within the same level of parentheses, functions are executed from left to right.

2. The function in the innermost parentheses is executed first, then the other functions are executed in order, working outward.

Two common mathematical functions are demonstrated in the syntax below:

```
DATA LIST FREE / v1 v2.
BEGIN DATA
1 2
-1 4
END DATA.
* Absolute value.
COMPUTE abs1 = ABS(v1).
* Square root.
COMPUTE sqrt2 = SQRT(v2).
FORMATS v1 to abs1 (F2.0).
LIST VAR = v1 abs1 v2 sqrt2.
```

Results from the **LIST** command are presented in Table 22.3. Mathematical functions are also available to find the modulus (remainder) of an argument, to round and truncate values, and to produce exponential, logarithms, and trigonometric values.

Table 22.3   Variables Created Using Mathematical Functions

V1	ABS1	V2	SQRT2
1	1	2	1.41
−1	1	4	2.00

Statistical functions are specified in the same way as arithmetic functions: They consist of the function name, followed by the argument(s) in parentheses. The following syntax demonstrates some common statistical functions:

```
DATA LIST FREE / v1 v2 v3 v4.
BEGIN DATA
1 2 3 4
```

```
END DATA.
* Calculating the sum.
COMPUTE sum1 = SUM(v1 to v4).
* Calculating the mean.
COMPUTE mean1 = MEAN(v1,v3).
* Finding the minimum value.
COMPUTE min1 = MIN(v2,v4).
* Finding the maximum value.
COMPUTE max1 = MAX(v1,v3).
FORMATS ALL (F3.0).
LIST VARS = sum1 to max1.
```

Results from the **LIST** command are presented in Table 22.4.

Table 22.4   Variables Created Using Statistical Functions

SUM1	MEAN1	MIN1	MAX1
10	2	2	3

MISSING VALUES IN NUMERIC OPERATIONS AND FUNCTIONS

Some common numeric calculations, such as adding numbers or taking a square root, can be done in SPSS either through a statement of arithmetic operations or through a mathematical function. If there are no missing data, either method will produce the same results. However, operations and functions differ in how they deal with missing data, and this can make a major difference in the outcome. Arithmetic operations will return a missing value if *any* of the variables in the equation are missing, while most functions will return a missing value for their results only if *all* the variables are missing. This difference is demonstrated in the following syntax:

```
DATA LIST / v1 to v3 1-6.
BEGIN DATA
1 2 3
1 2
END DATA.
COMPUTE add1 = v1 + v2 + v3.
COMPUTE add2 = SUM(v1 TO v3).
FORMAT ALL (F2.0).
LIST VARS = ALL.
```

Results from the **LIST** command are presented in Table 22.5. *Add1* is created by an arithmetic operation, and *add2* is created by a mathematical function. The first case has complete data, so the values for *add1* and *add2* are identical. The second case is missing on *v3*, so *add1* is missing and *add2* consists of the sum of *v1* and *v2*.

Table 22.5   Results of Operations and Functions Including Missing Data

V1	V2	V3	ADD1	ADD2
1	2	3	6	6
1	2	.	.	3

You can control whether functions will execute when some of their arguments are missing. For instance, you could decide that a function will be calculated only if at least eight of its arguments have valid values. This is specified with the **.n** suffix to function names, where **n** is the number of valid values required for the function to execute. The **COMPUTE** statement below will calculate the variable *newmean* only for cases that have valid values on at least eight of the variables *var1* to *var10*:

```
COMPUTE newmean = MEAN.8(var1 TO var10).
```

DOMAIN ERRORS

A domain error occurs when the result of a numeric expression is undefined for reasons other than missing data. Most domain errors are due to violations of mathematical rules, such as trying to divide a number by zero. When an arithmetic expression results in a domain error, SPSS issues a warning and the result of the expression is set to the system-missing value. A complete list of domain errors is available in the *SPSS 11.0 Syntax Reference Guide* (SPSS Inc., 2001), in the section on "Transformation Expressions."

A SUBSTRING-LIKE TECHNIQUE
FOR NUMERIC VARIABLES

Sometimes, numeric variables are used to store information in a manner analogous to string variables. One example is the variable computed to display missing-data patterns in Chapter 17. Another example is the variable *alcdays* in the 2001 BRFSS (Behavioral Risk Factor Surveillance System) survey (Centers for Disease Control, 2001). This **F3.0** variable holds the response to a question about how often the subject consumed alcohol. Some answered this question in terms of the number of *days per week* they drank, while others answered it in terms of the number of *days per month*. This information was captured in the left-most digit of *alcdays:* 1 indicated that the following two digits referred to days per week, while 2 indicated that the following digits referred to days per month (defined as the past 30 days).

To convert this variable to useful information, it is necessary to interpret the two right-most digits in terms of the meaning of the left-most. For instance, 107 would indicate a person who drank 7 days per week, which is 7/7 or 100% of the days, while 207 would indicate a person who drank 7 days per month, which is 7/30 or 23.3% of the days. The following code creates a small data set to illustrate how the information stored in *alcdays* can be used to compute the percentage of days a person drank alcohol:

```
DATA LIST / alcdays 1-3.
BEGIN DATA
107
210
105
200
END DATA.
IF alcdays GE 100 AND alcdays LE 107 drink = (alcdays-
   100) / 7.
IF alcdays GE 200 and alcdays LE 230 drink = (alcdays-
   200) / 30.
COMPUTE drink = DRINK * 100.
FORMAT drink (PCT6.1).
LIST VAR = ALL.
```

Results from the **LIST** command are presented in Table 22.6. The value of *drink* represents the percentage of days a person drank alcohol. For instance, the second case answered the question in terms of days per month and said he or she drank 10 days per month for a total of 10/30 or 33.3% of the days.

Table 22.6   Results of a Substring-Like Manipulation of a Numeric Variable

ALCDAYS	DRINK
107	100.0%
210	33.3%
105	71.4%
200	.0%

String Functions

T his chapter discusses functions for string variables in SPSS, including

○   The substring function

○   Concatenation

○   Searching for characters within a string variable

○   Adding or removing leading or trailing characters

○   Finding character strings identified by delimiters

All the functions discussed in this chapter operate on string variables. Numeric functions are discussed in Chapter 22, which also introduces the concept of a function, the parts of a function, and how functions are executed in SPSS.

THE SUBSTRING FUNCTION

The substring function allows you to extract a *substring* or string of characters from a string variable. This function is useful when dealing with string variables in which characters in different positions represent different types of information. For example, a hospital might identify a patient with a variable made up of the person's social security number plus a code indicating his or her health insurance plan. You may want to create two variables, one with the social security information and one with the health insurance information. This is accomplished in the following syntax:

```
* Creating new variables with the substring function.
DATA LIST / ID 1-12 (A).
BEGIN DATA
406615622101
100503425102
END DATA.
STRING ssn (A9) insur (A3).
COMPUTE ssn = SUBSTR(id,1,9).
COMPUTE insur = SUBSTR(id,10).
LIST VAR = ALL.
```

This syntax creates a data set with one variable, the 12-character string variable *id.* It then uses the substring function to write the first 9 characters of *id* into the string variable *ssn* and the last 3 characters into the string variable *insur.* The **SUBSTR** function has three arguments:

1. The variable from which the substring is to be extracted

2. The character where the substring begins

3. The character where the substring ends, which may be omitted if the substring runs to the end of the variable

The first substring function **SUBSTR(id,1,9)** tells SPSS to take a substring of the variable *id,* beginning at the first character and continuing to the 9th character. The second substring function, **SUBSTR(id,10)**, tells SPSS to take a substring of the variable *id,* beginning at the 10th character and continuing to the end of the variable. Output from the **LIST** command is presented in Table 23.1.

Table 23.1   Variables Created With the **SUBSTR** Function

ID	SSN	INSUR
406615622101	406615622	101
100503425102	100503425	102

CONCATENATION

Concatenation builds string variables by combining existing strings. To reverse the example above, you may have a file with variables representing people's social security numbers and insurance plans and wish to combine them into a single identification variable. The following syntax accomplishes this:

```
DATA LIST / ssn 1-9 (A) insur 11-13 (A).
BEGIN DATA
406615622 101
100503425 102
END DATA.
STRING id (A12).
COMPUTE id = CONCAT(ssn,insur).
LIST VAR = ALL.
```

The **CONCAT** function creates the variable *id* from the character strings of its arguments, the string variables *id* and *insur.* Output from the **LIST** command is presented in Table 23.2.

Table 23.2   Variable Created With the **CONCAT** Function

SSN	INSUR	ID2
406615622	101	406615622101
100503425	102	100503425102

Literal characters may be included as arguments to the **CONCAT** function. Continuing with the data set used to created Table 23.2, the following syntax will insert a dash (-) between the character strings *ssn* and *insur:*

```
STRING id2 (A13).
COMPUTE id2 = CONCAT(ssn,"-",insur).
LIST VAR = ssn insur id2.
```

Output from the **LIST** command is presented in Table 23.3.

Table 23.3   Concatenated Variable Including a Literal

SSN	INSUR	ID3
406615622	101	406615622-101
100503425	102	100503425-102

SEARCHING FOR CHARACTERS
WITHIN A STRING VARIABLE

The **INDEX** function searches for character strings within a string variable. It has two arguments:

1. The variable being searched

2. The character string searched for, enclosed in apostrophes or quotation marks

For instance, **INDEX(var1,'Smith')** searches the variable *var1* for the character string 'Smith'.

The **INDEX** function returns the value of the first position where the specified character string is found. If the string is not found, a value of 0 is returned. This function is used in the syntax below to search a file of patients and select those treated for ankle injuries:

```
DATA LIST / id (A3) injury (A30).
BEGIN DATA
01 Ankle Sprain
02 broken wrist
03 broken ankle
END DATA.
COMPUTE flag = INDEX(UPCASE(injury),'ANKLE').
FORMAT FLAG (F2.0).
LIST VAR = ALL.
SELECT IF FLAG NE 0.
LIST VAR = id injury.
```

The **UPCASE** function in the **COMPUTE** command converts the text being searched into uppercase letters and then matches it against the search term, which is also specified in all uppercase letters. This allows it to match both 'Ankle' in the first case and 'ankle' in the third case, which are different character strings in SPSS. The **COMPUTE** statement creates the variable *flag*, which will have a value of 0 if the search string is not found in the variable *injury*, and a number greater than 0 if it is found. Table 23.4 presents the results of the first **LIST** command, which displays the entire data set. The variable *flag* has the value of 0 for the second case because the search string was not found. Cases 1 and 3 have the value 1 and 8 for *flag*, respectively, indicating the first position where the search string was found for each case. Table 23.5 presents the results of the second **LIST** command, which includes only the cases with ankle injuries.

Table 23.4   Data File With Beginning of Character String Flagged

ID	INJURY	FLAG
01	Ankle sprain	1
02	Broken wrist	0
03	Broken ankle	8

Table 23.5   Display of Cases With Ankle Injuries

ID	INJURY
01	Ankle sprain
03	Broken ankle

ADDING OR REMOVING LEADING OR TRAILING CHARACTERS

Sometimes, you want to add or remove leading (left-most) characters from string variables. For instance, you may wish to increase the length of a field by adding leading zeros to it, or remove leading zeros in a field containing only digits. The following code demonstrates how a string variable may be padded with leading zeros using the **LPAD** (left-pad) function:

```
DATA LIST FREE / id (A1).
BEGIN DATA
1 2 3
END DATA.
STRING id3 (A3).
COMPUTE id3 = LPAD(id,3,'0').
LIST VAR = id id3.
```

The **LPAD** function has three arguments:

1. The name of the variable to be padded (in this case, *id*)

2. The total length of the string, including the padded characters (in this case, 3)

3. The character to used for padding (in this case, 0)

Results from the **LIST** command are presented in Table 23.6. The variable *id3* consists of the value of *id* plus enough leading zeros to give it a length of 3.

Table 23.6   Variable Padded With Leading Zeros

ID	ID3
1	001
2	002
3	003

Deleting leading characters in a string variable is similar to adding them. The following code demonstrates the use of **LTRIM** to remove leading zeros from the variable *id:*

```
DATA LIST FREE / id (A3).
BEGIN DATA
01 2 003 4 05
END DATA.
STRING idx (A3).
COMPUTE idx = LTRIM(id,'0').
LIST VAR = id idx.
```

The **LTRIM** functions has two arguments:

1. The variable to be trimmed (in this case, *id*)

2. The character to be trimmed (in this case, 0)

Results from the **LIST** command are presented in Table 23.7. The variable *idx* consists of the characters of the variable *id* minus the leading zeros.

Table 23.7   Variable With Leading Zeros Trimmed

ID	IDX
01	1
2	2
003	3
4	4
05	5

More complicated syntax is required to add leading zeros to a variable without increasing its length. The code below creates the **A3** variable *id3x*, which uses leading zeros consistently, from the **A3** variable *id*, which is inconsistent in its use of leading zeros:

```
DATA LIST FREE / id (A3).
BEGIN DATA
01 2 003 10 100
END DATA.
STRING id3x (A3).
COMPUTE idn = NUMBER(id,F3.0).
COMPUTE id3x = LPAD(LTRIM(STRING(idn,F3.0)),3,"0").
LIST VAR = id id3x.
```

The first **COMPUTE** statement converts the string variable *id* to the numeric variable *idn*, with format **F3.0**. The second **COMPUTE** statement performs the following tasks, reading the syntax from the innermost parentheses outward:

1. **STRING(idn,F3.0)**: Converts *idn* from a numeric to a string variable

2. **LTRIM(STRING(idn,F3.0))**: Trims leading blanks from the new string variable

3. **LPAD(LTRIM(STRING(idn,F3.0)),3,"0")**: Pads the new string variable with leading zeros to make it a character string of length 3

Results from the **LIST** command are presented in Table 23.8.

Table 23.8   Variable Trimmed Then Padded With Leading Zeros

ID	ID3X
01	001
2	002
003	003
10	010
100	100

The function **RTRIM** removes the right-most characters from a string variable. A typical use of **RTRIM** is to improve the appearance of a string variable created from several existing string variables. If some variables have fewer characters than their declared lengths, extra spaces will appear in the concatenated variable. The following code illustrates the creation of a new variable consisting of the first and last name of each case, first with extra spaces between the first-name and last-name fields *(name1)* and then using the **RTRIM** function to remove the extra spaces *(name2):*

```
DATA LIST FREE / lname (a15) fname (a10).
BEGIN DATA
Smith John
Doe Mary
END DATA.
STRING name1 name2 (A25).
COMPUTE name1 = CONCAT(fname,lname).
COMPUTE name2 = CONCAT(RTRIM(fname),' ',lname).
LIST VAR = name1 name2.
```

Results from the **LIST** command are presented in Table 23.9. *Name2* includes one space as a literal between *fname* and *lname*. If we had not added this space, the two variables would have run together (e.g., 'JohnSmith' for the first case). To trim any character other than a blank space, it is necessary to specify the character as the second argument to the **RTRIM** function. For instance, **RTRIM(var1,' 0')** would trim trailing zeros from *var1*.

Table 23.9　Concatenated Variable With and Without Extra Blank Spaces

NAME1		NAME2
John	Smith	John Smith
Mary	Doe	Mary Doe

FINDING CHARACTER STRINGS
IDENTIFIED BY DELIMITERS

It is possible to locate substrings that are identified by delimiters rather than by position. In the example below, the variable *id1* consists of a school code, a hyphen, and a pupil code. The syntax uses the hyphen to identify the two fields and writes their contents into the variables *school* and *pupil:*

```
* Finding the location of text strings identified by
  delimiters.
DATA LIST / id1 (A8).
BEGIN DATA
1-1
211-2
2-140
12-165
END DATA.
STRING school pupil (A3).
COMPUTE school = SUBSTR(id1,1,INDEX(id1,'-')-1).
COMPUTE pupil = SUBSTR(id1,INDEX(id1,'-')+1).
LIST VAR = id1 school pupil.
```

The first **SUBSTR** function begins reading at the first character of *id1* and continues until the last character before the hyphen, as indicated by **INDEX(id1,'-')−1)**. The second **SUBSTRING** function begins reading at the first character of *id1* following the hyphen, as indicated by **INDEX(id1,'-')+1)**, and continues to the end of the variable. Results from the **LIST** command are presented in Table 23.10.

Table 23.10 Variable-Length Substrings Identified by a Delimiter

ID1	SCHOOL	PUPIL
1-1	1	1
211-2	211	2
2-140	2	140
12-165	12	165

CHAPTER 24

Date and Time Variables

T his chapter explains how to use date and time variables in SPSS. Topics covered include the following:

○ How date and time variables are stored in SPSS

○ An overview of SPSS date formats

○ Reading dates with two-digit years in the correct century

○ Creating date variables with syntax

○ Creating date variables from string variables

○ Extracting part of a date variable

○ Doing arithmetic with date variables

○ Creating a variable holding today's date

○ Designating missing values for date variables

HOW DATE AND TIME VARIABLES ARE STORED IN SPSS

SPSS date and time variables are stored as floating-point numbers representing the number of seconds from 0 hours, 0 minutes, and 0 seconds on October 14, 1582, the date the Gregorian calendar was adopted. However, dates and times are usually entered and displayed in more familiar formats. The *SPSS 11.0 Syntax Reference Guide* (SPSS Inc., 2001) contains a detailed table of the time and date formats available in SPSS in the "Date and Time" section of the "Universals" chapter. Only the most commonly used formats will be discussed in this chapter.

AN OVERVIEW OF SPSS DATE FORMATS

This section discusses how to read date information into SPSS with the **DATA LIST** command and how to control the appearance of date variables with output formats. SPSS can read date information specified in many different ways. The following rules apply to reading date variables with the **DATA LIST** command:

1. The **FIXED** format must be used to read date variables.

2. The column width of date variables must be wide enough to accommodate the longest possible value of a date in a particular format.

3. Date variables must be identified by one of the date formats plus the variable width. Width information may be specified either by indicating the columns that contain the variable, as in the first example below, or as part of the date format, as in the second example:

```
DATA LIST / date1 1-9 (DATE).
```

or

```
DATA LIST / date1 (DATE9).
```

4. Date information can appear anywhere within a field, so leading or trailing blanks are not a problem.

5. Date variables containing day, month, and year information must use delimiters to separate those elements. The following characters are acceptable delimiters: dashes (-), commas (,), periods (.), slashes (/), and blanks ( ).

6. Months may be represented as numbers, Roman numerals, three-digit abbreviations, or may be fully spelled out.

7. Years may be entered with two or four digits. Two-digit years will be assigned to a century depending on the value of **EPOCH**, as discussed below.

8. Dates are displayed according to their output format, not necessarily how they were input.

These rules are demonstrated in the following syntax, which reads the same date values specified several different ways:

```
* Demonstration of different date input strings.
DATA LIST / date1 1-20 (DATE).
BEGIN DATA
1-OCT-02
01 / 10 / 2002
1 October 02
01 X 2002
01-oct-02
END DATA.
LIST VAR = ALL.
```

All cases will display as "01-OCT-2002." The input strings "1-OCT-02," "01/01/2002," and so on were converted to the numeric value 13252809600 and then displayed in the international date format **(DATE)** with a four-digit year (because 20 columns were allowed for the variables, which is sufficient to display the four-digit year).

One confusing point about date and time formats is that the input and output formats are sometimes different lengths. For instance, the minimum input length for a date in international format (dd-mmm-yy, for instance, 1-Jan-04) is 8, but the minimum output length is 9. This occurs because SPSS automatically increases the length of date and time formats to allow for the longest possible value. Any input formats specified by the programmer, however, should be long enough to allow for the longest possible value of a variable.

The same date information can be displayed many different ways, by changing the output format. This is demonstrated in the syntax below:

```
* Demonstration of different date output formats.
DATA LIST / refdate (DATE9).
BEGIN DATA
1-OCT-02
END DATA.
list var = refdate.
format refdate (adate8).
list var = refdate.
format refdate (date11).
list var = refdate.
format refdate (edate8).
list var = refdate.
```

```
format refdate (jdate7).
list var = refdate.
format refdate (sdate11).
list var = refdate.
```

Table 24.1 displays the appearance of the same date in different formats. Date formats specify both type (e.g., **ADATE** for American date, in which the month precedes the day) and width. The width controls whether two- or four-digit years are printed, so that using the **ADATE10** format in this example would cause *refdate* to display as 10/01/2002.

Table 24.1   Common SPSS Date Formats

Format	Appearance	Name of Format
date9	01-OCT-02	International date, 2-digit year
adate8	10/01/02	American date, 2-digit year
date11	01-OCT-2002	International date, 4-digit year
edate8	01.10.02	European date, 2-digit year
jdate7	2002274	Julian date
sdate9	2002/10/01	Sortable date, 4-digit year

READING DATES WITH TWO-DIGIT YEARS IN THE CORRECT CENTURY

When date variables are entered with two-digit years, SPSS has to assign them to a century. For instance, "01/01/01" could refer to January 1, 1901, or January 1, 2001. To make this assignment, SPSS uses a 100-year period whose default setting begins 69 years prior to the current date and ends 30 years after the current date. With this default setting, if you were entering data on January 1, 2001, the date 01/01/05 would be read as January 1, 2005, and the date 01/01/50 would be read as January 1, 1950.

To see what 100-year period is currently in use on your system, use the **SHOW EPOCH** command. If you want to change this period, use the **SET EPOCH** command, which specifies the first year of the 100-year span you wish to use. For instance, the command,

```
SET EPOCH 1910.
```

specifies the 100-year period 1910 through 2009. With this specification, the date 12/31/09 will be read as December 31, 2009, and the date 01/01/10 will be read as January 1, 1910. If dates in a data file span more than 100 years (for instance, 1800 to 2000), they must be entered with four-digit years in order to be read correctly.

CREATING DATE VARIABLES WITH SYNTAX

Sometimes, you need to create a date variable that was not in the original data file. For instance, you may want to create a variable holding the value of the date a research study began. The following syntax creates the date variable *refdate* with the value January 1, 1998:

```
COMPUTE refdate = DATE.DMY(01,01,98).
```

The function **DATE.DMY** is called an *aggregation function* because it combines several pieces of information (day, month, and year) into one date. **DMY** stands for "DayMonthYear" and specifies that the first argument refers to the day, the second to the month, and the third to the year. A number of other date aggregation functions are listed in the *SPSS 11.0 Syntax Reference Guide* (SPSS Inc., 2001), in the chapter on the **COMPUTE** command. The input values for an aggregation function can be variables instead of numbers. If the value of the variable *day* were 1, the value of the variable *month* were 5, and the value of the variable *year* were 1990, the command,

```
COMPUTE refdate = DATE.DMY(day,month,year).
```

would assign the date May 1, 1990, to the variable *refdate.*

CREATING DATE VARIABLES FROM STRING VARIABLES

Sometimes, a date field is stored as a string variable, for instance, when a data file created in one program has to be transferred to another. Two ways to create date variables from this type of string variable are presented below. Both methods create separate variables holding day, month, and year information. The first method then uses the **CONCAT** function to combine these variables into a date variable, as demonstrated in the following syntax:

```
* Creating a date variable from a string variable.
DATA LIST / olddate (A8).
BEGIN DATA
20021985
08101967
07021991
END DATA.
* Create separate day, month, and year variables.
STRING day month year(A2) new1 (A8).
COMPUTE day = SUBSTR(olddate,1,2).
COMPUTE month = SUBSTR(olddate,3,2).
COMPUTE year = SUBSTR(olddate,7,2).
* Concatenate month, day, and year.
COMPUTE new1 = CONCAT(month, "/",day, "/",year).
* Format the result to appear as a date.
COMPUTE newdate = NUMBER(new1,ADATE8).
FORMAT newdate (DATE9).
LIST VAR = ALL.
```

This syntax creates three new string variables to hold the day, month, and year elements, extracts the relevant information from *olddate*, and writes it to the new variables. It then creates the variable *new1* by concatenating the variables *month*, *day*, and *year*, separated by slashes, and converts the result to the numeric variable *newdate*. Finally, *newdate* is formatted as an international date with a two-digit year. Output from the **LIST** command is presented in Table 24.2.

Table 24.2　Date Variable Created From a String Variable

OLDDATE	DAY	MONTH	YEAR	NEW1	NEWDATE
20021985	20	02	85	02/20/85	20-FEB-85
08101967	08	10	67	10/08/67	08-OCT-67
07021991	07	02	91	02/07/91	07-FEB-91

The same results can be achieved by using the aggregation function demonstrated earlier. The following syntax uses the *day*, *month*, and *year* variables created in the program above:

```
* Using a date aggregation function.
* Convert the day, month, and year variables to numeric.
COMPUTE dayn = NUMBER(day,F2.0).
COMPUTE monthn = NUMBER(month,F2.0).
COMPUTE yearn = NUMBER(year,F2.0).
* Aggregate day, month, and year to a created a date
  variable.
COMPUTE newdate2 = DATE.DMY(dayn,monthn,yearn).
* Format the result as a date.
FORMAT newdate2 (DATE9).
EXE.
```

This syntax converts the variables *day, month,* and *year* to the numeric variables *dayn, monthn,* and *yearn*. It then creates the date variable *newdate2*, using those variables and the aggregation function **DATE.DMY**, and formats *newdate2* as an international date. The values of *newdate2* will be identical to those of *newdate* in Table 24.2.

EXTRACTING PART OF A DATE VARIABLE

Sometimes, you need to extract part of a date from an existing date variable. For instance, you could extract the day of the week from a variable holding the dates of medical appointments, to see whether some days are more heavily scheduled than others. SPSS provides a number of date extraction functions, which are listed in the *SPSS 11.0 Syntax Reference Guide* (SPSS Inc., 2001), in the **COMPUTE** chapter. Several date extraction commands are illustrated in the code below:

```
* Demonstration of date extraction functions.
DATA LIST / date1 (DATE11).
BEGIN DATA
11-Feb-1995
END DATA
* Extract the month.
COMPUTE month = XDATE.MONTH(date1).
* Extract the year.
COMPUTE year = XDATE.YEAR(date1).
* Extract the day of the week.
COMPUTE daywk = XDATE.WKDAY(date1).
* Extract the day of the month.
COMPUTE daymth = XDATE.MDAY(date1).
FORMAT month to daymth (F4.0).
```

Daywk and *month* can be formatted so they are spelled out, as in the following syntax:

```
FORMAT month (MONTH15).
FORMAT daywk (WKDAY10).
LIST VAR = ALL.
```

Output from the **LIST** command is presented in Table 24.3.

Table 24.3 Variables Created Using SPSS Date Extraction Functions

DATE1	MONTH	YEAR	DAYWK	DAYMTH
11-Feb-1995	FEBRUARY	1995	SATURDAY	11

DOING ARITHMETIC WITH DATE VARIABLES

You can do arithmetic with dates in SPSS, such as calculating the number of days between two dates. However, the results of such a calculation will be in seconds, and usually we want to convert them to more meaningful units, such as days or years. This conversion can be carried out either by performing an arithmetic function or using an automatic-conversion function.

Using the first approach, you can convert seconds to days by dividing by 86400, the number of seconds in a day. Similarly, you can convert days to years by dividing by 365.25, the number of days in a year (the quarter day is to allow for leap years). Converting seconds to years requires dividing by (365.25 * 86400). These techniques are demonstrated in the following syntax:

```
* Using arithmetic to convert seconds to days and
  years.
DATA LIST / date1 (DATE11) date2 (DATE11) date3
  (DATE11).
BEGIN DATA
11-Feb-199513-FEB 199515-SEP-1996
END DATA.
COMPUTE days1 = (date2-date1) / 86400.
COMPUTE years1 = (date3-date1) / (365.25 * 86400).
LIST VAR = days1 years1.
```

The variable *days1* will have the value of 2.00, and *years1* of 1.59. You can also convert seconds to days using the SPSS date conversion function **CTIME.DAYS**. For instance, we can compute *days1* and *years1* with the following syntax:

```
COMPUTE days1 = CTIME.DAYS(date2-date1).
COMPUTE years1 = (CTIME.DAYS(date3-date1)) / 365.25.
```

The results will be the same as above: *days1* = 2.00, *years1* = 1.59.

Because *days1* and *years1* are the results of arithmetic procedures, they are in the default **F8.2** format. The fractional parts of these numbers can be eliminated by using the **TRUNC** (truncation) function to drop the noninteger portion of the numbers and using the **FORMATS** function to display the numbers without decimal places. It is also possible to format variables to appear without decimals but without specifying truncation, in which case decimal values greater than .5 will be rounded up to the next integer. The difference is demonstrated in the following syntax:

```
DATA LIST FREE / var1 var2.
BEGIN DATA
1.3 1.3
1.5 1.5
1.8 1.8
END DATA.
LIST VAR = ALL.
COMPUTE tvar1 = TRUNC(var1).
FORMATS var2 tvar1 (F2.0).
LIST VAR = ALL.
```

Results of the **LIST** command are presented in Table 24.4. *Var1* and *var2* have the same value for each case, but *var1* is displayed in the default **F8.2** format and *var2* in the **F2.0** format. *Tvar1* is truncated and displayed in the **F2.0** format. *Var2* and *tvar1* appear identical for the first case because *var2* holds the value 1.30 but does not display the decimal part, while *tvar1* holds the truncated value 1. This is not true for the second and third cases, which have values of 1.50 and 1.80 for *var1*. When 1.50 and 1.80 are formatted to appear without decimal places in *var2*, they are rounded up to the next integer, in this case, 2, because their decimal value is .5 or greater. When these values are truncated in *tvar1*, the decimal places are simply dropped, so *tvar1* has the value of 1 for both variables. Truncation changes the stored value of a variable, not merely its appearance. Once a value is truncated, the parts that have been dropped cannot be restored.

Table 24.4   Rounding and Truncation Contrasted

VAR1	VAR2	TVAR1
1.30	1	1
1.50	2	1
1.80	2	1

Often, you want to add some fixed length of time to an existing date. For instance, you may want to create a new variable that is one day later than the value stored in a data variable in your file. Since a day in SPSS terms is the number of seconds in a day (86,400), adding a day to a date variable means adding 86,400 to that variable. The following syntax creates new variables one day *(plusday)* and one week *(plusweek)* later than the date stored in the variable *date1:*

```
DATA LIST / date1 (DATE11).
BEGIN DATA
11-May-2000
END DATA.
COMPUTE plusday = date1 + 86400.
COMPUTE plusweek = date1 + (7 * 86400).
FORMAT plusday plusweek (DATE11).
LIST VARS = ALL.
```

The value of *plusday* will be "12-MAY-200," and the value of *plusweek* will be "18-MAY-2000."

CREATING A VARIABLE HOLDING TODAY'S DATE

The system variable **$TIME** holds the value of today's time and date, according to your computer's internal clock. As discussed in Chapter 19, you cannot display the value of a system variable directly, but you can use the **XDATE.DATE** function to extract the date information from this system variable and store it in another variable. The value of the new variable may be displayed, used in calculations, and so on. This is demonstrated in the following syntax:

```
DATA LIST / bdate (DATE11).
BEGIN DATA
04-JUN-1955
10-AUG-1962
END DATA.
* Make a variable holding today's date.
COMPUTE today = XDATE.DATE($TIME).
* Calculate age as of today.
COMPUTE age = CTIME.DAYS(today-bdate) / 365.25.
COMPUTE age1 = TRUNC(age).
FORMAT today bdate (DATE11) age1 (F2.0).
LIST VAR = ALL.
```

Results from the **LIST** command are presented in Table 24.5. This program reads in a data set with two cases and one variable, *bdate* (representing someone's birthdate). It uses the **XDATE.DATE** function to extract the value of today's date from the system variable **$TIME** and store it in the variable *today*. It then calculates the variable *age* for the two cases by subtracting *bdate* from *today* and converting the result to years. The result is displayed both as an **F8.2** variable *(age)* and truncated *(age1)*. Of course, the variable *today* will depend on the date when you run this syntax, so the values of *age* and *age1* will also differ.

Table 24.5   Results of Calculations Using Today's Date

BDATE	TODAY	AGE	AGE1
04-JUN-1955	20-MAR-2004	48.79	48
10-AUG-1962	20-MAR-2004	41.61	41

DESIGNATING MISSING VALUES FOR DATE VARIABLES

Sometimes, a default date is entered into a database to signify that the information was not available. For instance, "Jan. 1, 1900," might be entered in the field for a person's birthdate if that information is unknown. You may want to declare this value as missing so it will not be used in computations or reports. There are two ways to accomplish this: Recode this value as system-missing, as in the first example below, or declare this value to be user-missing, as in the second example below. The code below will substitute the system-missing value for the date value corresponding to January 1, 1900, for the variable *bday:*

```
IF bday = DATE.MDY(1,1,1900) bday = $SYSMIS.
```

Once this code is executed, the date information will be permanently deleted from cases holding the value corresponding to January 1, 1900.

To declare a date as missing without deleting its value, you must find the numeric value of that date and specify that value as user-missing, with the **MISSING VALUES** command. Both steps are demonstrated in the following syntax:

```
DATA LIST / bdate (DATE11).
BEGIN DATA
04-JUN-1955
1-JAN-1900
END DATA.
* Find the numeric value of 1-JAN-1900.
COMPUTE missdate = DATE.DMY(1,1,1900).
FORMAT missdate (F13.0).
LIST VAR = missdate.
* Declare the numeric value of 1-JAN-1900 as missing.
MISSING VALUES bdate (10010390400).
FREQ VAR = bdate.
```

This syntax reads in a data set with two cases and one date variable, *bdate.* It uses the **COMPUTE, FORMAT**, and **LIST** commands to find the numeric value of the date 1-JAN-1900, then declares this as a missing value for *bdate.* Output from the **FREQUENCIES** command, presented in Table 24.6, demonstrates that the date value representing January 1, 1900, was declared user-missing but the value itself was not deleted from the variable *bdate.*

Table 24.6   Data Set With User-Missing Data for a Date Variable

		BDATE			
		Frequency	Percent	Valid Percent	Cumulative Percent
Valid	04-JUN-1955	1	50.0	100.0	100.0
Missing	01-JAN-1900	1	50.0		
Total		2	100.0		

Part V

Other Topics

Automating Tasks Within Your Program

This chapter discusses how to use repeating functions in SPSS. Topics discussed include:

○ Vectors

○ The **DO IF** command structure

○ The **DO REPEAT** command structure

○ The **LOOP** command structure

VECTORS

A vector in SPSS is a set of variables identified as a group and assigned a name. Variables defined as a vector can be referenced by the name of the vector, and individual variables within a vector may be referenced by the vector name plus an index number indicating their position within the vector. Vectors are often used within repeating structures because they allow a program to use a group of variables without having to name every variable in that group.

The variables named in a vector may be preexisting or created by the **VECTOR** command. The first **VECTOR** command below creates five new variables, named *vector1* to *vector5*, while the second **VECTOR** command associates five existing variables with the vector name *vect2:*

```
VECTOR vector (5).
VECTOR vect2 = v1 to v5.
```

The syntax below demonstrates the use of the **VECTOR** and **LOOP** commands:

```
DATA LIST / v1 to v5 1-10.
BEGIN DATA
1 2 2 1 2
2 1 1 2 1
END DATA.
FORMATS v1 to v5 (f1.0).
LIST VAR = ALL.
VECTOR vect = v1 TO v5.
LOOP #i = 1 TO 5.
DO IF vect(#i) = 2.
COMPUTE vect(#i) = 0.
END IF.
END LOOP.
LIST VAR = ALL.
```

The **VECTOR** command associates the vector name *vect* with the variables *v1* through *v5*. The **LOOP** command that follows takes advantage of the fact that SPSS treats the variables named in a vector as *elements* of the vector, which may be identified by the vector name plus an index number. For instance, the first time the **LOOP** executes, the value of *#i* is 1, so the **DO IF** and **COMPUTE** commands refer to variable *vect(1)* or *v1*, the first element in the vector *vect*. The second time the loop executes, these commands refer to *vect(2)* or *v2*, and in the fifth and final loop, they refer to *vect(5)* or *v5*. Results of the first **LIST** command, which display the data set as read by the **DATA LIST** command, are presented in Table 25.1. The **DO IF** and **COMPUTE** commands within the **LOOP** structure recode the values of 2 to 0 for variables *v1* to *v5*. This recoding is reflected in the results from the second **LIST** command, presented in Table 25.2.

Table 25.1   Data Set Before Recoding

V1	V2	V3	V4	V5
1	2	2	1	2
2	1	1	2	1

Table 25.2   Data Set After Recoding

V1	V2	V3	V4	V5
1	0	0	1	0
0	1	1	0	1

It is possible to specify the format for variables created with the **VECTOR** command, as in the following code:

```
VECTOR str(3,A1) num(2,F1.0).
```

This syntax will create three string variables of length 1, named *str1*, *str2*, and *str3*, and two numeric variables of length 1, named *num1* and *num2*.

Although SPSS recognizes variables as elements of a vector within *transformations*, it is not valid for *procedures* such as **FREQUENCIES**. For instance, you cannot get a frequency table for the variables *v1* to *v5* with the command,

```
FREQ VAR = vect.                              [WRONG]
```

or a frequency table for *v3* with the command,

```
FREQ VAR = vect(3).                           [WRONG]
```

THE DO IF COMMAND STRUCTURE

The **DO IF** command structure is an extension of the **IF** command discussed in Chapter 21. We refer to the **DO IF** *command structure* because **DO IF** is one of a series of commands that are used together: **DO IF**, **ELSE IF**, and **END IF**. The **DO IF** command structure allows you to perform a series of transformations conditional on the values of a series of logical expressions. This is demonstrated in the following code:

```
DO IF (age GE 18 and age LT 30).
COMPUTE agecat = 1.
ELSE IF (age GE 30 and age LT 50).
COMPUTE agecat = 2.
ELSE IF (age GE 50).
COMPUTE agecat = 3.
END IF.
```

The conditional statements in this syntax (**DO IF, ELSE IF**) include logical statements that are evaluated for their truth or falsity, as discussed in Chapter 21. If the logical statement is true, the transformation is executed and SPSS will skip over the rest of the commands in the **DO IF** structure. If the logical statement is false, the transformation is not executed and SPSS will evaluate the next logical statement in the command structure. If none of the conditions are true, SPSS will reach the **END IF** statement without having executed any of the **COMPUTE** statements and the case will be assigned the system-missing value for *agecat*. The **END IF** command is required: Failure to include it will result in an "unclosed **DO** loop," and the syntax will not execute.

THE DO REPEAT COMMAND STRUCTURE

The **DO REPEAT–END REPEAT** command structure is an efficient way to perform transformations on a group of variables, as illustrated in the syntax below:

```
DO REPEAT v = var1 TO var20.
COMPUTE v = 0.
FORMAT v (F1.0).
END REPEAT.
```

This syntax sets values of the variables *var1* to *var20* to 0 for all cases, a process also known as "initializing *var1* to *var20* to 0." The same result could have been realized by a series of **COMPUTE** statements, but the **DO REPEAT** structure is more efficient because it uses the *stand-in variable v* to represent *var1* to *var20:* The transformations specified for *v* will be executed on *var1* to *var20*.

Not all SPSS commands can be used within a **DO REPEAT** structure. *The SPSS 11.0 Syntax Reference Guide* (SPSS Inc., 2001) has a complete list of available commands in the chapter on the **DO REPEAT** command. Those used most often are data transformations; missing-value declarations; print, write, and format commands; and the **LOOP** and **DO IF** structures. Variable and value labels commands cannot be executed within the **DO REPEAT** structure and neither can descriptive and statistical procedures such as **FREQUENCIES, MEANS**, and **REGRESSION**.

A typical use of the **DO REPEAT** command structure is to create a series of indicator variables from a single categorical variable. An *indicator* or *dummy* variable is a variable that indicates the presence or absence of some characteristic. Often, dummy variables are coded as 0 or 1, although other coding schemes may also be used. Dummy variables are used in procedures such as regression, where the use of numerically coded nominal variables would be misleading. The following syntax creates four indicator variables, *ethnic1* to *ethnic4*, using the information from the categorical variable *ethnic*:

```
DATA LIST FREE / ethnic (F1.0).
BEGIN DATA
1 2 3 4
END DATA.
DO REPEAT eth = ethnic1 to ethnic4 / x = 1 to 4.
COMPUTE eth = 0.
DO IF ethnic = x.
COMPUTE eth = 1.
FORMAT eth (F1.0).
END IF.
END REPEAT.
EXE.
LIST VAR = ALL.
```

The **DO REPEAT** structure uses two stand-in variables: *eth*, which stands for the new variables *ethnic1* to *ethnic4*; and *x*, which will take the values 1 to 4 and controls which of the variables *ethnic1* to *ethnic4* will be coded with a 1. For instance, the value of *ethnic* for the first case is 1, so the value of *ethnic1* will be 1 and the value of *ethnic2, ethnic3*, and *ethnic4* will be 0. For the third case, the value of *ethnic* is 3, so the value of *ethnic3* will be 1 and *ethnic1, ethnic2*, and *ethnic4* will have a value of 0. This may be clarified by Table 25.3, which presents the results of the **LIST** command.

Table 25.3   Indicator Variables Created With the **DO REPEAT**
Command Structure

ETHNIC	ETHNIC1	ETHNIC2	ETHNIC3	ETHNIC4
1	1	0	0	0
2	0	1	0	0
3	0	0	1	0
4	0	0	0	1

Distinct variable names can be used in a **DO REPEAT** structure, also. For instance, the following **DO REPEAT COMMAND** could be substituted into the previous program, and the results would be the same except that the variables created would be named *White, Black, Hispanic,* and *Other:*

```
DO REPEAT eth = White Black Hispanic Other / x = 1
  to 4.
```

THE LOOP COMMAND STRUCTURE

The **LOOP–END LOOP** command structure directs SPSS to perform the commands within the structure repeatedly until some limit on the number of repetitions is reached. A simple **LOOP** structure was demonstrated in the section on vectors in this chapter. There are several ways to specify how many times a loop should be repeated. The simplest is to rely on the maximum number of loops allowed by the current setting on your computer. You can see what this setting is with the command **SHOW MXLOOPS** and set it to some value (10 in this example) with the command,

```
SET MXLOOPS = 10.
```

The **MXLOOPS** setting prevents the creation of an "infinite loop," in which the program keeps executing a loop forever because the programmer did not include code to tell it when to stop.

Usually, programmers do not depend on the **MXLOOPS** value, but control the number of iterations with an *index* or *counter* variable. An index variable is a variable included in the **LOOP** statement that will be incremented once with each repetition of the **LOOP**. A *scratch variable* is often used for this purpose because it does not need to become a permanent part of the data set. Use of an index variable *(#i)* is demonstrated in the syntax below:

```
COMPUTE sum = 0.
LOOP #i = 1 to 6.
COMPUTE sum = sum + 1.
END LOOP.
```

The variable *#i* begins with a value of 1 and is incremented (in this case, increased by the default of 1) after each repetition of the loop. The **LOOP** command specifies that the loop will be repeated while *#i* has a value from 1 to 6, which is equivalent to a logical condition that is true when *#i* has a value in that range. When the value of *#i* becomes 7, SPSS will exit the **LOOP** structure and resume reading syntax following the **END LOOP** command. The number of loops can also be stored in a variable, as demonstrated in the following code:

```
COMPUTE exit = 6.
COMPUTE sum = 0.
LOOP #I = 1 to exit.
COMPUTE sum = sum + 1.
END LOOP.
```

The number of loops is controlled by the value of the variable *exit*, in this case, 6. This method of control has the advantage that the **LOOP** syntax can be used unchanged, while the number of loops is controlled by a variable outside its structure.

The number of executions may also be controlled by **IF** statements within the **LOOP** structure. The following syntax places the test condition in the **LOOP** statement so the logical condition will be tested before each execution of the loop:

```
COMPUTE x = 0.
LOOP IF (x LT 5).
COMPUTE x = x+1.
END LOOP.
```

This loop will execute five times, and the final value of **x** will be 5. At the beginning of the sixth repetition, the condition **(x LT 5)** will be false, so SPSS will pass control to the syntax following the **END LOOP** command. Similar results can be achieved by including the test condition at the end of the loop, as in the following syntax:

```
COMPUTE x = 0.
LOOP.
COMPUTE x = x+1.
END LOOP IF (x = 5).
```

This loop will also execute five times. After the fifth repetition, the condition **(x = 5)** will be true, so the **END LOOP** command will be executed and control will pass to the syntax following it.

A **LOOP** structure can be used with an **INPUT PROGRAM** structure to create a data set. This technique was demonstrated in Chapter 18 to generate random variables from a specified distribution. Here, we use the same technique to create a data set that includes a variable containing values for all the days within a specified time period, for use with a longitudinal project:

```
* Generate a file with all the dates from 1-Feb-1999
  to 31-Jan-2001.
* Loop is 0 to 1095, will create 1096 consecutive
  dates.
INPUT PROGRAM.
LOOP dayid = 0 TO 1095.
COMPUTE n_date = DATE.MDY(2,1,1999) + (86400*dayid).
FORMAT n_date (DATE11).
END CASE.
END LOOP.
END FILE.
END INPUT PROGRAM.
EXE.
FORMAT dayid (F4.0).
MEANS ALL/CELLS = COUNT MIN MAX.
```

This program uses the index *dayid*, which begins with a value of 0 and ends with a value of 1,095, causing the **LOOP** to execute 1,096 times (the number of days between 1-Feb-1999 and 31-Jan-2001). Each repetition of the loop adds one day (86,400 seconds) to the beginning value of *n_date* (1-Feb-1999), so the final date generated will be 31-Jan-2001. This syntax creates a file with 1,096 cases: The first has the value 0 for *dayid* and 01-FEB-1999 for *n_date*, the second has the value 1 for *dayid* and 02-FEB-1999 for *n_date*, and so on, as seen in Table 25.4. Output from the **MEANS** command demonstrates that the number of cases and date range generated are correct.

Table 25.4   Means Table for a File of Dates Created With **INPUT PROGRAM**

	DAYID	N_DATE
N	1,096	1,096
Minimum	0	01-FEB-1999
Maximum	1,095	31-JAN-2002

CHAPTER 26

A Brief Introduction to the SPSS Macro Language

This chapter discusses the SPSS macro language. Topics covered include:

○ The parts of a macro

○ Different ways to declare arguments in a macro

○ How to control the macro environment

○ How to find more information about macros

This chapter introduces the SPSS macro language. Many SPSS users are unaware that the macro language exists, and others may feel it is too difficult for them to learn. The purpose of this chapter is to break through those initial barriers by introducing the concept of the macro language, presenting the basic techniques necessary to write simple macros, and directing interested readers to sources of further information.

The SPSS macro language is a programming language that makes it possible to write, name, and recall self-contained sections of code called *macros*. The macro language has two main uses:

1. To automate procedures done repeatedly

2. To write algorithms to calculate statistics, generate distributions, and so on that are not included in any of the SPSS prewritten routines

The macros presented in this chapter are simple because their purpose is to introduce the macro language. More complex macros can be found in the sources listed at the end of this chapter. As with SPSS syntax, the most efficient way to learn to the macro language is by examining and altering macros written by others.

THE PARTS OF A MACRO

SPSS macros begin with the command **DEFINE** and end with the command **!ENDDEFINE**. The first line of a macro includes the command **DEFINE**, the *name* of the macro, and the definition of any *arguments* to the macro, within parentheses. Empty parentheses must be included in this line even if the macro does not include arguments. *Arguments* in this context are the names used to refer to the variables or sets of variables used within a macro. A macro may have multiple arguments, and each argument may consist of multiple variables. The *macro body* consists of the lines between the **DEFINE** and **!ENDDEFINE** commands. A *macro call* is a line of syntax outside the macro that begins with the name of the macro followed by the arguments and variables to those arguments, if required. When a macro call is executed, the macro facility *expands* it, that is, substitutes the commands contained within the macro for the name of the macro, using the variables named in the macro call in place of the argument names in the macro. These commands are then executed as if they had been written into the syntax at that point, using the current active file. A few notes about macros:

1. Macro names are often preceded by the exclamation point (!), in order to differentiate them from other variable names or keywords. Other than this, the same rules apply as do for SPSS variable names, as discussed in Chapter 20.

2. Macro keywords and commands are preceded by the exclamation point (!).

3. Arguments referred to in the macro body must be preceded by exclamation points.

4. If a macro name appears anywhere in SPSS syntax, even in a comment prefaced by an asterisk (*), it may be invoked (i.e., called and executed). For this reason, the /* */ style of commenting (discussed in Chapter 7) should be used when a comment includes the name of a macro.

5. The command structure **BEGIN DATA–END DATA** cannot be used in a macro.

MACROS WITHOUT ARGUMENTS

Not all macros require arguments. The syntax below creates a macro named *!demogr* and associates the variables *age, race, gender, income,* and *education* with it, so that a procedure that refers to *!demogr,* in this case the **FORMAT** and **LIST** commands, will be executed on those variables:

```
DATA LIST FREE / age race gender income educ.
BEGIN DATA
25 1 1 20 12
40 02 0 35 16
END DATA.
DEFINE !demogr () age race gender income educ.
!ENDDEFINE.
FORMAT !demogr (F4.0).
LIST VAR = !demogr.
```

The results of the **LIST** command are presented in Table 26.1. These results are identical to those that would have been produced with the command,

```
LIST VAR = age race gender income educ.
```

Table 26.1   LIST Table Produced With a Macro Call

AGE	RACE	GENDER	INCOME	EDUC
25	1	1	20	12
40	2	0	35	16

MACROS WITH ARGUMENTS

Macros that use arguments can perform operations on variables specified outside the macro. Note that a single argument can refer to multiple variables, as in the syntax below:

```
* Macro with arguments.
DATA LIST FREE / var1 to var4.
BEGIN DATA
```

```
3 2 4 3
2 1 2 4
2 1 1 1
3 4 4 5
END DATA.
DEFINE !stats1 (varlist = !TOKENS(4))
FREQ VAR = !varlist
   / STATS = MEAN STDDEV
   / FORMAT = NOTABLE.
!ENDDEFINE.
* Call this macro.
!stats1 varlist = var1 TO var4.
```

The definition of the macro *!stats1* names one argument, **varlist**, and specifies with the **!TOKENS(4)** keyword that **varlist** will consist of four variables to be named in the macro call. A **TOKEN** in this context means something to be passed from one part of the program to another, in this case a variable to be passed from the macro call to the macro. The body of the macro consists of a **FREQUENCIES** command that will be performed on **varlist**. The macro call consists of the macro name (**!stats1**), the argument (**varlist**), and the variables that will constitute **varlist** for this execution of *!stats1* (**var1 TO var4**). The macro call will produce the results in Table 26.2.

Table 26.2   Frequencies Table Produced With a Macro Call

		VAR1	VAR2	VAR3	VAR4
N	Valid	4	4	4	4
	Missing	0	0	0	0
Mean		2.500	2.000	2.7500	3.2500
Std. Deviation		.57735	1.41421	1.50000	1.70783

Macros can also use *Keyword* arguments, which means that user-defined names are assigned to arguments specifying the role they play in the macro. This is demonstrated in the following syntax:

```
* Macro with keyword arguments.
DEFINE !cross1 (row = !TOKENS(1)
   / col = !TOKENS(1)).
CROSSTABS TABLES = !row by !col
   / CELLS = COUNT ROW.
```

```
!ENDDEFINE.
* Call this macro.
!cross1 row = var1 col = var2.
```

The macro definition assigns the keywords **row** and **col** to the arguments to be used in the cross-tabulation procedure. Each consists of one variable to be specified on the macro call statements, as specified by **!TOKENS(1)**. The keywords are used in the macro call to identify which variable should be used in each part of the cross-tabulation procedure. Execution of the macro call will produce a cross-tabulation table of *var1* by *var2*.

SPECIFYING ARGUMENTS BY POSITION

Arguments may be specified by position within the macro call. The macro *!cross2* below achieves the same results as *!cross1* using positional specification:

```
* Macro with positional arguments.
DEFINE !cross2 (!POSITIONAL !TOKENS(1)
    / !POSITIONAL !TOKENS(1)).
CROSSTABS TABLES = !1 by !2
    / STATS = CHISQ
    / CELLS = COUNT ROW.
!ENDDEFINE.
* Call this macro.
!cross2 var1 var2.
```

The keyword **!POSITIONAL** in the macro definition tells SPSS that the variables used in the macro body will be identified by their positions in the macro call. The first-named variable is identified in the macro body as **!1** and will be the row variable in the cross-tabulation table, and the second-named variable is identified as **!2** and will be the column variable. In the macro call, the first-named variable is *var1* and the second-named is *var2*, so this macro call will produce a cross-tabulation table of *var1* by *var2*.

MACROS USING A FLEXIBLE NUMBER OF VARIABLES

There are three ways to use arguments in macros without specifying the number of variables associated with them:

1. **!ENCLOSE**, which includes the variables enclosed within specified symbols

2. **!CHAREND**, which includes the variables up to a specified character

3. **!CMDEND**, which includes the variables up to the end of the macro call

The following three syntax examples achieve the same results using these three methods of argument definition. The first example illustrates the use of **!ENCLOSE**:

```
* Macro with flexible number of variables.
DATA LIST FREE / var1 var2.
BEGIN DATA
1 1 1 0 0 1 0 0 0 1
END DATA.
* Macro using !ENCLOSE.
DEFINE !means1 (!POSITIONAL !ENCLOSE('[',']')).
MEANS !1 / CELLS = COUNT MEAN.
!ENDDEFINE.
* Call this macro.
!means1 [var1 var2].
```

The macro definition specifies square brackets ([]) as the symbols that define which variables named in the macro call will be used in the macro. The **!1** in the macro body is optional in this case because only one group of variables is used. If there were several groups of variables, they would be referred to in the macro body as !1, !2, and so on, as in the macro *cross1* above. Results from the macro call are presented in Table 26.3.

Table 26.3   Means Table Produced With a Macro Call

	VAR1	VAR2
N	5	5
Mean	.4000	.6000

The next macro uses the same data set and specifies the arguments with **!CHAREND**:

```
* Macro using !CHAREND.
DEFINE !means2 (!POSITIONAL !CHAREND('/')).
MEANS !1 / CELLS = COUNT MEAN.
!ENDDEFINE.
* Call this macro.
!means2 var1 var2 /.
```

The argument statement identifies the slash (/) as the symbol that defines the variables to be used. All variables named in the macro call, up to the first instance of this symbol, will be used in the macro. Results from this macro are the same as those presented in Table 26.3. If the call statement had been written as follows,

```
!means2 var1 / var2.
```

only *var1* would be used.

The third example also uses the same data set and defines the arguments with **!CMDEND**:

```
* Macro using !CMDEND.
DEFINE !means3 (!POSITIONAL !CMDEND).
MEANS !1 / CELLS = COUNT MEAN.
!ENDDEFINE.
* Call this macro.
!means3 var1 var2.
```

Results will be the same as those presented in Table 26.3.

Different argument specifications can be combined. For instance, the following macro combines the **!CHAREND** and **!CMDEND** specifications:

```
* Macro illustrating two types of argument
  specification.
DATA LIST FREE / var1 var2 var3.
BEGIN DATA
1 2 3
1 2 3
1 1 1
2 2 1
END DATA.
```

```
DEFINE !view (!POSITIONAL !CHAREND('/')
   / !POSITIONAL !CMDEND).
FREQ VAR = !1.
MEANS !2 / CELLS = COUNT MEAN.
!ENDDEFINE.
* Call this macro.
!view var1 / var2 var3.
```

The argument statement specifies that variables named on the macro call statement, up to the slash (/), constitute the group identified in the macro body as **!1.** The second group of variables, identified in the macro body as **!2,** includes all variables from the slash to the end of the macro call. This macro will produce a frequency table for the first group of variables (in this case, *var1*) and a means table for the second group of variables (in this case, *var2* and *var3*).

CONTROLLING THE MACRO LANGUAGE ENVIRONMENT

There are four settings related to the macro language that may be listed with the **SHOW** command and changed with the **SET** command (discussed in Chapter 4). **MPRINT** has a value of **YES** or **NO** and regulates whether macro commands will be listed after expansion. **MEXPAND** has a value of **ON** or **OFF** and controls whether macros will be expanded. **MNEST** specifies the maximum number of levels of nesting allowed within macros, and **MITERATE** specifies the maximum number of loop iterations within macro expansion. The following command will get information about your current settings:

```
SHOW MPRINT MEXPAND MNEST MITERATE.
```

MEXPAND must be set to **ON** in order for macros longer than one line to be executed; if for some reason it is set to **OFF** in your system, you can reset it with the command,

```
SET MEXPAND ON.
```

SOURCES OF FURTHER
INFORMATION ABOUT SPSS MACROS

This chapter has only been able to introduce macros and give a few simple examples. To use the macro language efficiently, the programmer will have to progress beyond the elementary level. An essential source of information about the macro language is the *SPSS 11.0 Syntax Reference Guide* (SPSS Inc., 2001), which discusses macros primarily in the Appendix, "Using the Macro Facility," and in the chapter on the **DEFINE–!ENDDEFINE** command structure. Two other books can be recommended: *SPSS Programming and Data Management* (Levesque, 2003) and *Next Steps with SPSS* (Einspruch, 2004).

There are many sources of SPSS macros. First, the books named above include examples of macros with explanations of how they work. In addition, many SPSS macros are available on the World Wide Web. A number are available from SPSS Inc.: You can find macros on the SPSS Web site by searching for the term "macro" or "!ENDDEFINE" from the technical support page (SPSS Technical Support). Many examples of macros, some with detailed explanations of how they work, can be found on the Raynald Levesque site (Raynald's SPSS Page). A Web search on "SPSS macros" or "SPSS AND !ENDDEFINE" will locate many more pages containing SPSS macros.

CHAPTER 27

Resources for Learning More About SPSS Syntax

Becoming an SPSS programmer is an ongoing learning process. Resources to aid in this process are discussed in this chapter, including:

○ Books

○ Web pages

○ Mailing lists

BOOKS

SPSS Inc. produces several useful resources for the programmer. The most important is the *SPSS 11.0 Syntax Reference Guide* (SPSS Inc., 2001), which is available both as a printed book and as an electronic file in Adobe Acrobat format. This guide is a reference book that contains detailed information about SPSS commands and about the SPSS system in general. The electronic version is particularly useful because you can search the text for character strings using keyboard commands or the menu choices **Edit**, **Find**. Other resources are the earlier versions of the SPSS manuals, which contain many examples of syntax and annotated output. One "classic" manual to which many programmers still refer is the third edition of the *SPSS-X User's Guide* (SPSS Inc., 1988). SPSS Inc. also offers a number of training courses, including *Syntax I: Introduction to SPSS Syntax* and *Syntax II: Programming With SPSS Syntax and Macros,* and sells the guides to these courses through their Web site (SPSS Training).

Several other books may be useful to the SPSS programmer. *SPSS Programming and Data Management* (Levesque, 2003) includes many examples of syntax, and the coverage of macros is particularly good. *Next Steps with SPSS* (Einspruch, 2004) also includes many examples of syntax. *Using Multivariate Statistics* (Tabachnick & Fidell, 2001) is an intermediate statistics textbook that includes many examples of SPSS syntax and annotated output, primarily to demonstrate statistical procedures. The *SPSS 11.0 Guide to Data Analysis* (Norusis, 2002) demonstrates many analytical techniques using the menu system but can be used to generate and save SPSS syntax using the techniques discussed in Chapter 5.

There are many books that discuss computers and programming in general. *The Philosophical Programmer* (Kohanski, 1998) discusses programming for readers without technical backgrounds. *Learning Computer Programming* (Farrell, 2002) is more technical but presupposes no background in programming. The *Free On-Line Dictionary of Computing* (FOLDOC) contains a wealth of technical and historical information about computers and programming.

WEB PAGES

SPSS Inc. has a Web page at http://www.spss.com/. The organization of this site changes frequently, so it may be necessary to search the site to find particular sections. One useful feature for programmers is the searchable database of questions and answers regarding SPSS (SPSS Technical Support).

A number of institutional and personal Web pages include SPSS syntax. One very useful page is Raynald's SPSS Page (Levesque), maintained by the author of *SPSS Programming and Data Management* (Levesque, 2003), mentioned above. This Web page includes a FAQ (Frequently Asked Questions) page for SPSS; a searchable archive of SPSS programs, macros, and scripts; and a page devoted to SPSS beginners.

University Web sites are another good source of code. Only two of the best sites are mentioned here. The Web site of the University of California at Los Angeles includes a wealth of searchable SPSS information (UCLA Academic Technology Services). The University of Texas Web site includes answers to a number of questions regarding SPSS (University of Texas).

Many other Web pages that include examples of SPSS code and programming advice may be found by searching with a Web search engine, such as Google, on terms such as "SPSS syntax."

MAILING LISTS

The SPSSX-L mailing list is an active email list for SPSS users, managed through the University of Georgia (UGA) Web site. List members post SPSS problems and solutions, and statistical topics are often discussed as well. Instructions on subscribing and a searchable list archive are available online (University of Georgia).

References

Adobe Systems Inc. (n.d.). *Download Adobe reader.* Retrieved March 15, 2004, from http://www.adobe.com/products/acrobat/readstep2.html.

Centers for Disease Control. (2001). *BRFSS survey data.* Atlanta, GA: Author.

Einspruch, E. L. (2004). *Next steps with SPSS.* Thousand Oaks, CA: Sage.

Farrell, M. E. (2002). *Learning computer programming: It's not about languages.* Hingham, MA: Charles River Media.

FOLDOC: The free on-line dictionary of computing. (n.d.). Retrieved March 15, 2004, from http://foldoc.hld.c64.org/index.html.

Kohanski, D. (1998). *The philosophical programmer: Reflections on the moth in the machine.* New York: St. Martin's.

Levesque, R. (n.d.). *Raynald's SPSS page.* Retrieved March 15, 2004, from http://pages.infinit.net/rlevesqu/.

Levesque, R. (2003). *SPSS programming and data management: A guide for SPSS and SAS users.* Chicago: SPSS Inc.

Little, R. J. A., & Rubin, D. B. (2002). *Statistical analysis with missing data* (2nd ed.). Hoboken, NJ: Wiley.

Norusis, M. (2002). *SPSS 11.0 guide to data analysis.* Upper Saddle River, NJ: Prentice Hall.

Raudenbush, S. W., & Bryk, A. S. (2002). *Hierarchical linear models: Applications and data analysis methods* (2nd ed.). Thousand Oaks, CA: Sage.

SPSS Inc. (n.d.). *About SPSS Inc.: Corporate history.* Retrieved March 15, 2004, from http://www.spss.com/corpinfo.history.htm.

SPSS Inc. (n.d.). *Software and solutions.* Retrieved March 15, 2004, from http://www.spss.com/products/.

SPSS Inc. (1988). *SPSS-X User's Guide* (3rd ed.). Chicago: Author.

SPSS Inc. (2001). *SPSS 11.0 syntax reference guide.* Chicago: Author.

Stone, R., & Fox, J. (Eds.). (1997). *Statistical computing environments for social research.* Thousand Oaks, CA: Sage.

Tabachnick, B. G., & Fidell, L. S. (2001). *Using multivariate statistics* (4th ed.). Boston: Allyn & Bacon.

UCLA Academic Technology Services. (n.d.). *Resources to help you learn and use SPSS.* Retrieved March 15, 2004, from http://www.ats.ucla.edu/stat/spss/.

University of Georgia. (n.d.). *Archives of SPSSX-L@LISTSERV.UGA.EDU.* Retrieved March 15, 2004, from http://listserv.uga.edu/archives/spssx-l.html.

University of Texas. (n.d.). *Frequently asked questions and answers.* Retrieved March 15, 2004, from http://www.utexas.edu/cc/faqs/stat/index.html#SPSS.

Index

NOTE: SPSS keywords are presented in all capital letters ($CASENUM). SPSS commands are presented in all capital letters and boldface type (**ADD FILES**). For commands used frequently (e.g., **DATA LIST**), only principal text references are cited.

About the Author

Sarah Boslaugh, PhD, has more than 20 years of experience working in data management and statistical analysis. She has worked as an SPSS programmer and statistician in many different settings, including education, health care, government, and the insurance industry.

Dr. Boslaugh received her PhD in research methods and evaluation from the City University of New York and is currently a Senior Statistical Data Analyst in the Department of Pediatrics at the Washington University School of Medicine in St. Louis. Her research interests include multilevel modeling, geographic information systems, and measurement theory.